500

THE PRODIGY

THE OFFICIAL STORY
ELECTRONIC PUNKS
MARTIN ROACH

D0912583

THE EARLY YEARS
1988–1994

Published in 2010 by
INDEPENDENT MUSIC PRESS
Independent Music Press is an imprint of I.M. P. Publishing Limited
This Work is Copyright © I. M. P. Publishing Ltd 2010

The Prodigy – Electronic Punks
by Martin Roach

British Library Cataloguing-in-Publication Data.
A catalogue for this book is available from The British Library.

ISBN 978-906191-17-7

Cover Design by Fresh Lemon.
All photos except press shots by Sharon Thornhill.

Independent Music Press
P.O. Box 69, Church Stretton, Shropshire SY6 6WZ

Visit us on the web at: www.impbooks.com

For a free catalogue, e-mail us at: info@impbooks.com
Fax: 01694 720049

Printed and bound in the UK

THE PRODIGY

ELECTRONIC PUNKS
THE EARLY YEARS
1988-1994

by Martin Roach

Independent Music Press

ACKNOWLEDGEMENTS

Many thanks to Liam, Keeti and Keith – over the years since this book was written you have all been constantly willing to help me and support my books, even when your crazy schedules barely allow it. I am extremely grateful, thank you sincerely.

A huge thanks must also go to John Fairs who, despite being the busiest person I've ever met, always returns my calls, always goes that extra mile to help me and is a true gentleman; I'd also like to thank Leeroy, Mike Champion, Sharon Thornhill, Linz, Dave Clarke and Dave Hanley.

CONTENTS

FOREWORD

We never had a masterplan of where we were gonna take this. People have to remember we were just ravers going out partying and all we were interested in at the beginning was getting into parties for free. Playing gigs at the parties was just enabling us to do that. All we knew was that we were as good as the bands we were seeing playing. And we knew we could be up there doing it next to them.

It was an amazingly exciting feeling to be a part of a culture that was happening right there and then; we hadn't borrowed something, people weren't reliving a previous culture, it was brand new. The rave scene was happening right at that exact moment – and we were right in the middle of it.

When I signed my first record deal, to be honest it didn't really register with me. All I was interested in was having DJs play my tunes. If a record deal gave me that, great, and if it also gave me some money to buy some more equipment then even better. In fact, I didn't actually want to do an album, I thought that might be selling out, there weren't really bands around at that time doing albums in the scene, so it didn't necessarily feel right.

When you are young, you are very naïve and very open, but at the same time that can mean you are very unaffected by outside forces. I found it very easy not to fall into that, not to be influenced by stuff, I just did my thing, I was totally naïve to … to anything really. That created a really high creative input. As time went on, that aspect obviously became less and less and you have to work really hard to keep that. It's very hard to keep hold of, even if you are the most underground person, situations change, things change around you, it's very difficult, you constantly have to rebel.

One thing I would like to point out that influenced me musically is a label that I owe a lot to – in terms of our sound – Shut Up And Dance Records. They aren't talked about much but I give them respect. Outside dance it was Public Enemy and my hip-hop roots. But in dance that label was underground, a proper London sound, the first people to do breakbeat and house/dance music. Many people might have credited us to be the first people to do that, but actually it was Shut Up And Dance.

The early days were a blur of constant gigging. We've never really stopped touring. It's always been our thing. Maybe for some bands touring is something you have to do to sell records, but for us it was always the main thing. Doing gigs. And we were writing the music for the gigs. That's still what we do now. In fact, it's even more important than ever. Back then, you could survive by not playing live so much as long as the DJs were playing your tunes. But as soon as we had any success, underground DJs stopped playing us. So we just gigged and gigged and gigged. That path connected us to the people out there, it was the biggest buzz.

I'm very proud of those first two albums. To me it's almost two different bands. There are some similarities, obviously the beliefs are still the same across the two records. When I listen to the first album, it is a snapshot of exactly what was going on at that time. I listen to *Experience* and I hear so many ideas in each track, so many melodies, like every twenty seconds a new idea comes in. That was the way it was, the hyper state of the music, of the rave scene, that is what it was all about – how many riffs and how much excitement and stimulation you can fit in one track from different sounds.

I'd get back home ideally before my dad got up, so as not to disturb him! Usually I'd be really fired up from the night and get straight on the equipment and try to lay down some of the inspirations or sounds I'd remember from the night before.

I always had the ability – and still do – to get excited about the smallest detail. I can get excited about just one sound – such as a drum sound for example – it's crazy, but I can get excited about doing an entire song around one singular sound. I have never lost that. I still get that feeling when I hear a noise or sound and can build up a tune from just that.

The process was simpler in many ways back then. Firstly, the equipment was so simple: you really had to stretch your imagination and also the equipment could only handle so much information, you really had to get as much down as you could on those tracks, there was limited sample time on these machines, so you had to make the most of what you'd got.

Quite soon after that first record I got quite disillusioned with the scene and fed up, it totally changed. People were sucking off the scene just to make money, putting on shit events and rippin' people. I was thinking of a way that the band could survive and push forward. Then we heard Rage Against The Machine whilst in LA and that opened our minds up to a different sound and feeling, it was like Public Enemy with the raw rock power energy. That led on to *Jilted*. That album was also a reaction to what was going on in the dance music scene – for example, 'Poison' was a reaction to everyone turning up the tempo on jungle to ridiculous speeds, crazily fast, so we were like, 'Fuck you, we are doing something slow and your gonna love it!'; we also hated the Euro dance thing that was getting in people's ears so much, so I wrote 'No Good' to try to destroy that. I think it's quite a forward-thinking album, whereas the first record was a pure snapshot. *Jilted* was the moment which pushed things in a different direction, it was a much darker approach. That was the product of an underlying anger in the band. That feeling that people didn't necessarily understand us, of not wanting to be labelled, just wanting to push things further, do something different. That just fueled us. We were being labelled a techno band and all that kind of shit, so I brought guitars into the mix because it was a new sound and energy for me, I knew it would piss the purists off. That's the point, this band has always been anti-purist , we still are, make something different for fuck's sake … I'm very proud of that record.

Reading this book again just confirms what I remember, I can see the hunger and self-belief. It's much more difficult for new bands to do that these days, because so much hinges around money, but when we were first out there, we didn't have that, we were signed to an independent, we turned so much stuff down all the time, we just didn't give a fuck. We'd say, 'That's not right for us, we can't do that.' But there was no masterplan, we made it up as we went along, it wasn't like we were aiming to sell millions of records, we were just like, 'There's a right way of doing this and there's a wrong way. We've got to live with ourselves and we know if something is cool or not.'

We knew so much about the scene we were from and therefore we knew what sounded original, what would or wouldn't hit because we were ravers ourselves. We were testing the music on ourselves to see what would buzz. We were four geezers taking Es and all that, and even when all that slowed down, we still knew when something hit the spot. I guess once it's in you … you know.

Self-belief and hunger are crucial. Obviously you have to have a talent and a creativity, a flare. But self-belief and hunger … that's what it's all about. To this day, these are the two factors that drive us, a total understanding of *not giving a fuck about anyone else*.

Liam Howlett, July 2010.

INTRODUCTION

"This is the best punk album I've heard in years."
This was the first thing I said on meeting a 22-year-old
Liam Howlett in the front room of his manager's Essex
house. I was talking about his debut album *Experience*,
hailed by many as the highlight of the rave culture,
a definitive piece spewed out from the underground of
one of Britain's last great illicit subcultures. I was a year
older, a punk publisher putting out books about bands
I loved with little regard for commerce or credibility. My
musical tastes were similarly insular; I'm pretty sure my
CD collection wouldn't have impressed many journalists
or critics, but I just liked to listen to what I liked to listen
to. And in 1992, that was *Experience* by The Prodigy.

I'd read all the reviews of course, about how Liam
had variously 'saved' or 'killed' rave; I'd seen the band at
a number of unusual 'venues', I'd buzzed with the energy
of the seething debut 'What Evil Lurks' and when they
infected the charts with their single 'Charly', I was
delighted for them and bemused by the chants of 'selling

out'. My view was this: how could they 'sell out' rave when *Experience* was obviously a punk masterpiece?

I knew Liam had prowled around raves and clubs with his rough-cut but brutally brilliant mix tapes. I was more than aware of the musical context. But he wasn't a rave musician; maybe as a commercial entity he was birthed by that phenomenon, but he was certainly not confined by it. The subsequent history of the band unarguably tells us that much.

For me, this was pure punk. Liam was punk. He was barely out of his teens when he wrote the majority of that first album. He knew pretty much no one in the music business. He didn't particularly want to know anyone either. He went to raves, he went home and he wrote music. Long before people were buying Pro Tools and releasing 'home-made' albums, Liam Howlett was handing out tapes – old school audio-cassettes – at raves to anyone who would listen. In so doing, he pre-dated the digital revolution (that put the established recording industry to the sword) by years. It was, to use his own future words, a one-man army. And wasn't that what punk was all about? Not the safety-pins, the caricatures in Trafalgar Square, the frayed bondage trousers, the granny-baiting headlines … it was all about *DIY*.

His writing process back when I first met him was crushingly economic; one of the label executives from XL told me that the tapes he delivered were as good as ready to go – so he really was writing the music, recording it and effectively mainlining it to the listener's ears. And with that directness came a certain authenticity, an honesty. It was just Liam's genius spilled out on to the stereo.

Of course, as The Prodigy evolved into a genuine genre-straddling beast that headlined festivals all over the world, the recording process became elongated. By his own admission, there have been times when this original brevity of creation has become too protracted – most obviously for the fourth album, *Always Outnumbered Never Outgunned* – but at the point I wrote this book, this was not the case.

It seemed to me that it wasn't just the way Liam recorded his material that was punk; it was the sound too. It was visceral, it was brutal and it was unashamedly brazen, utterly confrontational. His trusty Roland W30 (rather than the ubiquitous Ataris of the day) enabled him to create and sample sounds that fuelled his artistic fire. Liam still uses this keyboard on occasion to this day. Back then in the early 1990s, it gave him a palette of beats that to most people's ears sounded like a revolution.

Suitably moved to want to write about this eclectic young musician, I decided to get in touch. On the inner sleeve of early copies of his debut album, Liam's manager – the inimitable Mike Champion – gave out his phone and fax number. So I called him. Mike himself answered. I told him I was a big fan of Liam's music, that I thought he was going to be a massive star and that when he was, I'd like to write a book about him. I have no idea what Mike was thinking while I said this but he couldn't have been more friendly. To this day he remains one of the most amiable characters in the business. He said it sounded like a great idea and why didn't I travel down to his Essex home to have a bite to eat and chat some more.

The following week I caught the train and when I got

there Mike's assistant picked me up in a big Essex boy racer car – I don't recall the exact make, but I do recall it was *fast*. We drove to Mike's house and I was put into a front room with a cup of tea. Then Liam walked in. He had a cold and was carrying a snotty handkerchief, and he apologised profusely for his sniffles as he sat down. He was rakish thin, with piercing eyes and a hard cut jaw line. He looked very cool. After brief introductions, he asked me why I liked his album. And that's when I told him it was my favourite punk album of recent times.

This was backed up by the band's live show which even when it was predominantly at 'rave' or dance venues, always had a rock edge to it. There might have been no guitars in these early days and certainly no human drummer, but Prodigy gigs always felt like exactly that – a gig. In the early days, the Keith Flint 'Firestarter' persona was some way off but even then, both he and Maxim were crucial pieces of the jigsaw. And Leeroy Thornhill too, who sadly made an exit in 1999, was also compelling with his elongated dance moves and larger-than-life presence. Watching the band's two frontmen evolve into arguably the most unique pairing in music has been a privilege.

Even as their profile escalated ever higher until they were one of the world's biggest bands, Liam, Maxim and Keith always supported my books and helped me whenever I asked; in 1994 when I was compiling a book about my favourite songwriters – *The Right to Imagination and Madness* – Liam happily gave up his time to speak to me again, this time more specifically about the actual process of writing (and he had another cold that day too!). It was a fortuitous conversation as he had recently completed the masterpiece that was *Music For The Jilted Generation*; within months the music world would hear that record and his life would never be the same again. I have attached that interview in the back of this book as an appendix, to give a more close-up insight into the maverick genius behind The Prodigy's music.

Fast-forward to when Liam was writing the group's third album, *The Fat of the Land*, we were simultaneously working on a photo book for the band. He was living in a modest but very cool coach house in Braintree and I would go round on a Tuesday and Thursday night to design the book and go through photos with him, Keith and Maxim. The phone seemed to be constantly ringing with offers, approaches and record labels all anxious to get his signature on a contract. Liam was so laid-back about it all it was startling. We talked about the cries of 'sell-out' which still harped on and he was very philosophical. "I just want to get my music out to as many people as possible, man. Simple as." Eventually he signed to Maverick, co-founded by Madonna no less. The album he was writing in that coach house would later enter the *Billboard* charts at Number 1 as well as topping the charts in more than 25 countries, selling over 10 million copies in the process. So job done then.

One day in the early months of 1996, more than a year after this book had originally been released, I was in the East End studio of a music magazine photographer. There was a mezzanine level above the main room and I was up there, flicking through black and white shots of Kurt Cobain while waiting for The Prodigy to arrive for a shoot. This was just before the band released a new single called 'Firestarter' on to an unsuspecting world.

There was a click as the studio door opened and I looked over the balcony. Below me I saw Keith Flint walk in, sporting his brand new 'Firestarter' haircut. It was the closest I have ever felt to being in the same room as a rabid tiger. He was literally prowling, an animalistic presence that was genuinely shocking. He looked absolutely incredible. Maxim sloped in next, arguably the coolest man on the planet, all silver teeth and deep black tattoos. And then came Liam. He shuffled in, looked up, said, "Alright man" and turned the stereo up to ten.

At that moment, looking and sounding like they did, it was obvious that something massive was about to happen to The Prodigy. The band that had crawled out from the underground in the period covered by this book was no more; I knew then that nothing would ever be the same for them again. When they left that photo studio that afternoon, just around the corner was the multi-million-selling behemoth that was *The Fat of the Land* and the 'Firestarter' was about to terrify Middle England. Back then, Liam was literally as raw as the proverbial diamond in the rough, writing music, playing music and following his own path, regardless of fashion, acclaim or sales.

And he is exactly the same today.

Ditto Maxim and Keith.

And you can't get much more punk than that.

CHAPTER 1

"Hip-hop was about standing in the corner being bad and looking cool, but this new scene was just about being part of something."

Liam

"I think it's best that you leave." The man was standing alarmingly close, his breath warm and fetid on Liam's face, as he angrily spat out his feelings. "You're from Essex, this isn't your area, so get out now." As he spoke, he opened a back door to the club and gestured for Liam and his three friends to leave. It was a bad end to a brief and uneasy night. They had come to north-west London after an invite from one of the hip-hop club's DJs, but as soon as they entered the small venue, it was clear that they would not be welcome. Within twenty awkward minutes, they were hustled out into a back room and told to empty their pockets, and when they scornfully declined there was a brief and angry confrontation as furtive hands tried to rifle through their jackets. They pushed the grabbing hands away but their defiance did them little good – they were still forced to leave. Angry, but with no real choice, the foursome headed back through the dimly lit side streets of north London to the gold Cortina in which they had come. As they did, one of Liam's friends pulled out a handgun which he had recently bought on the black market, and talked about going back to the club to return the threats they had just been subjected to, but it was pointless, there would only be more trouble. By the time the car doors had clanged shut and the cold engine had stuttered into life, the atmosphere was thick with disappointment, and for the entire journey home there was a disenchanted silence. When the car took the signposts for Braintree, Liam wondered if he would ever be respected and at home in the hip-hop scene.

Six days later, a seventeen-year-old Liam Howlett was in his own car, a battered Ford Escort, heading for The Barn in Rayne, on the way to his first rave. The venue itself was exactly that – an old barn, complete with wooden beams and high ceilings which made for an exceptional atmosphere. Essex had always been a stronghold for innovative dance music clubs, with the 1970s seeing Canvey Island's Goldmine and Rayleigh's Pink Toothbrush leading the jazz-funk and Brit soul booms. Similarly in the late 1980s, The Barn very quickly established itself as one of the premier clubs in Britain, and during its time saw PAs by all the biggest acts of the scene, including the likes of N Joi, Shades Of Rhythm,

Guru Josh, and Lil' Louis; in addition, the resident DJ was Mr.C, who went on to enjoy considerable mainstream success with The Shamen. Even so, despite the club's celebrated reputation, as Liam walked up to the main door he still sensed the same trepidation that had accompanied him on most of his outings to hip-hop clubs recently – this was, after all, a new thing for him, how would the regulars react?

He needn't have worried. Within half an hour of being in The Barn, Liam had found his musical home, and the memories of that first night are still vivid in his mind.

"It was incredible. Me and a friend went because we had heard all about this rave thing – my old school friends were already into it, but I just thought it was a drugs phase they were going through. Until then I had only ever smoked a few puffs of weed which I thought was quite heavy, so all this acid seemed a bit serious to me.

"I watched the people taking acid and they looked okay on it, so I took half a tab. All I can remember after that is that the club just sparkled." The entire evening flew past in what felt like five minutes – the music made him buzz and he thought the feeling of his first acid trip accentuated the whole experience. When the last record finally cut out, Liam was left with a huge grin spread across his face. He stumbled out of the club still in a daze, and walked around the town centre for a few hours; unlike the violent night a week earlier, the only paranoia he felt was the fear that he might not come down off the trip before he finally went back home. The next day, he knew he was converted. "I thought it was the bollocks, such a different experience from what I had become used to. Hip-hop was such an exclusivist, pretentious scene, and to a certain extent, that always excluded white bands. Then to experience something like that first night at The Barn was such a stark contrast, I really loved the music and the whole vibe. I had never been into dancing that much, but it didn't matter here because you could just smile and jump around and really enjoy it, you didn't have to dance properly. The next week though I didn't take acid at all, because I wanted to check it out more clearly, and I found that the buzz was exactly the same for me. I really got into it then."

*   *   *

During the middle of 1988, a new musical form began sweeping through the UK's clubland with its hypnotic beats and new age drug culture – Acid House. The origin of the term is unclear, although many people claim it was inspired by the group Phuture's 'Acid Trax' single of 1987. The musical origins of the form were also somewhat difficult to identify. Many saw it as evolving from the musical mecca of Chicago. Others said it hailed from Detroit, and laid the credit at the feet of people such as Juan Atkins, Derrick May, Kevin Saunderson, and other innovative DJs and musicians. Whatever its actual origins, the new minimalist Acid House had many musical cousins, but its mind-altering frequencies, relentless rhythms, unconventional structures and off-beat soundscapes imbued it with a weirdness and unorthodoxy all of its own. Whilst house music tempered its rhythmic obsession by incorporating more melodies and harmonies, Acid House pursued rhythm to new extremes, using the technology that had broken the mould of traditional live instrument music, and in the process producing beats that could never be simulated by flesh and blood musicians. The music soon crossed the Atlantic, and was introduced to Britain through the massive illegal warehouse parties that formed the foundation for what became known as rave. With the so-called smart bars selling high energy, strictly non-alcoholic, caffeine-full drinks to fuel the marathon dancing, the culture rapidly adopted a recycled hippy mantra, and its 'love vibe' and benign communality created what came to be called The Summer Of Love. The media did not like it one bit (*Top of the Pops* even banned some 'acid' tracks) nor did the authorities and the older generation, but this attempted criminalisation only served to increase the rebellious flavour, and hence the popularity, of the massive all-night parties. Ironically, many of the people who now condemned rave as barbaric, mindless, repetitive, and nihilistic were the same people who had grown up in the 1960s with the same criticisms being levelled at their very own amphetamine stutter of 'My Generation'. The mainstream snub for the 'smiley culture' later took on a more determined edge in October of 1989 when special anti-drug squads were set up to combat the phenomenon, but for now the baggy jeans and long haired 'ravers' ran free across the country. Pirate radio stations filtered new material out from under the noses of the media, and the sheer scale of some all-nighters (frequently running to tens of thousands) meant that the authorities had seemingly little power to stop them. In the south-east, the M25 motorway became celebrated on thousands of flyers for illegal parties, as it cut off a neat section of south-western Essex which became a haven for the phenomenon. The early parties were secretive affairs with people being given phone numbers to call, or meetings to attend at service stations along the M25, whereupon they could find out the secret location of that night's party. The almost complete lack of reliable or accurate media documentation further heightened the pervading sense that this was an utterly underground experience.

★   ★   ★

Liam's final conversion to rave had taken some time. When the summer of 1988 had arrived and the nation had been swept up in the communal euphoria of Acid House, Liam had actually barely noticed. He was too busy with his hip-hop band, Cut To Kill, and the early simplistic acid music he heard on pirate radio held no appeal. For some time now he had been a hip-hop fanatic, but his musical background was a litany of various styles. His first ever record was *Ska's Greatest Hits* which his dad had obligingly bought for him. Bands like The Selector and The Specials appealed to the youngster's interest in street level music. That autumn, when Liam graduated to the local comprehensive school, he was exposed to many new styles of music and spent hours around his friends' houses swapping records and plundering their vinyl collections. One such session unearthed a record by Grandmaster Flash And The Furious Five, the New York-based act who mixed their encyclopaedic knowledge of black American music with impressive turntable skills to great effect with tracks such as 1984's 'The Message'. Liam was dumbstruck by this material and over the coming months dived into this new genre, buying what records he could afford as his appetite for musical knowledge became voracious. His interest was further fuelled when the hip-hop film *Beat Street* arrived in the UK, and by now Liam was an ardent fan of the whole scene, the scratching, the mixing, the breakdancing, the graffiti, everything. Yet, despite his interest in all the elements of the new scene, including the fashion and clubs, he always gravitated most strongly towards the music itself.

Having enjoyed lengthy classical piano lessons as a kid, Liam inevitably began to nurture his own musical ideas, and with the use of a friend's old four-track recorder he tried a few primitive mixes in his bedroom. Despite the crude nature of the mixes, Liam revelled in the challenge, and vowed to save enough money to buy his own turntable. "Once I had messed with my friend's four-track I had to get one of my own, so I took this job on a building site in the summer holidays, hoping to save enough money to get my own turntable. It was such hard work, and I was just this skinny little kid running up and down these ladders all day. I was returning home every night absolutely shattered, and only getting fifty quid a week. At the end of the first week I remember getting to the top of this ladder with a big bucket full of concrete in my hand and suddenly my arm started to shake uncontrollably, I just couldn't hold it, I was in agony. It was early in the day and I had weeks to go before I would have enough money for my turntable, and I thought, 'Fuck this, I don't want to do this'. Then this picture of two decks in the corner of my bedroom appeared in my head, so somehow I carried on, wobbling my way to the top of this ladder."

On the last day of the holidays, Liam walked off the building site and straight into the local music shop, where he immediately spent all his hard-earned savings on two modest turntables. Every night he would come back from school, run upstairs and spend hours practising on the decks. It was now that Liam felt confident enough to approach the aforementioned Cut To Kill, the local hip-hop outfit whom he had seen and liked and he was duly accepted on board as their second DJ, alongside an MC, a beatbox guy and the original DJ. Liam's career in Cut To Kill was to last two years, during which time he became a DJ of some local repute. In the early days, despite all the band still being at school, they played quite regularly at small local venues such as the YMCA at Chelmsford, attracting reasonable crowds of 150 people or more with the photocopied flyers they designed for each show. They were not exactly prolific, but when the band did gig Liam loved it. Once the group left school, things started to become a little more serious. With his A-level in Graphic Design, Liam secured a job at one of the many London free magazines, a publication called *Metropolitan*, where he befriended the art director and entertained him with stories of Cut To Kill's activities. One day, Liam was taken aback when the director offered to manage the band and invest £4000 in an album recording session and production schedule. The four friends were duly consigned to a local studio, where they recorded and cut twelve tracks; unfortunately, the entire budget for the project was spent in the studio, leaving little for promotion or release. Undeterred, the band and manager sent out fifty copies of the debut album to prospective record companies, agents and other industry figures. They did not receive any serious interest.

The demoralising dearth of interest in the band's album coincided with the period of repeated snubs by the hip-hop underground scene, culminating in the recent violent night at the London club. Therefore, Liam's first rave a week later came at a vulnerable time when his enthusiasm for hip-hop was quickly wilting – it was soon completely extinguished for the time being, when the other members of Cut To Kill went to Tam Tam Records and signed a record deal but excluded Liam from the arrangement completely. Surprisingly, Liam was relatively unconcerned by this move. Besides, it gave him the opportunity he had been increasingly craving for to get on with writing his own material. When he found out about this, he finally turned his back on the hip-hop scene and headed straight for The Barn.

★   ★   ★

At the age of 16, James Brown was convicted of petty theft and sent to the Alto Reform School, where his days were spent slopping out and avoiding the institutionalised violence. His future looked as grim as the outside world, which was embroiled in the Second World War. When Leeroy Thornhill reached the same age, he spent all day watching videos and listening to records of the same James Brown, who had by now been making legendary music for over thirty years and was firmly established as 'The Godfather Of Soul'. Brown's dancing footwork and speed fascinated Leeroy – whilst Liam was on the other side of town immersing himself in the musicality of hip-hop, Leeroy veered towards the dancing. He loved the music, of course, but dance was how he got his buzz. Having been through a brief dalliance with Mods, parkers and Two Tone, Leeroy picked up on the nascent electro scene and spent many long nights in town with his sheet of lino and bottle of Mr. Sheen, breakdancing with his friends, before riding home on his BMX. When electro was usurped by hip-hop, Leeroy was again immediately taken, but never lost sight of his original influences such as rare groove and soul, and he began frequenting local clubs where he would dance to tracks by artists like Maceo, George Clinton, Stevie Wonder and, of course, James Brown. Unfortunately, his local social life was dealt a severe blow two years after leaving school when his job took him two hundred miles west to the spa town of Bath. It was whilst he was working here as an electrician that Leeroy missed the start of a new scene for the first time in his young life – acid house had arrived. Not wanting to miss out, Leeroy drove home one weekend and joined a group of friends for an evening of acid house at The Barn. The club itself seemed okay, but for once Leeroy did not appear to be comfortable with the style of dancing – to him everyone appeared to be just running on the spot and when he tried it his body could not latch on to the beats of the sparse music. He wasn't getting a buzz, not from the music, not from the people and not from the dancing. Leeroy was not impressed: "It wasn't very interesting. I had never done any drugs so that was all a bit strange. On top of that, and odd as it sounds, I just thought, 'This is white man's music.' All I could see were these people at The Barn, all white, all dressed the same, all dancing the same. There was nothing there for me to lock on to and dance to."

He continued working in Bath for a further nine months and every two weeks he would return home, but still remained unimpressed by his friends' tales of the infant rave scene. However, by the summer of 1989, the supremely minimalist musical nature of acid had developed into something a little more varied, with a greater variety of beats and layers of rhythms starting to be mixed in with the original, more sparse material. Suddenly Leeroy could see something fresher and more exciting than previously, and he decided to try a rave once more. His new hopes seemed to be doomed when he again tried and failed at the odd running style of dance, so he sat down next to a speaker, miserable and dejected. Almost as an afterthought, he swallowed the tab of ecstasy that he had been given by a friend, and suddenly his whole body seemed to spark into life: "That was it, I was off!! The combination of this massive house sound system and the drug just took me over. I jumped up and started dancing and didn't stop for three years.

The Prodigy

I got on the E buzz and that was it for a good while, because you knew what you were taking and you only needed one tab." Leeroy had found a scene where he could dance all night, then go on to another party and dance through until the morning – within a matter of weeks he was hooked on the scene: "At that point it was fantastic – the whole E buzz of meeting so many people and being friendly with them was so amazing, so communal, there was none of this standing with your arms folded in the corner with your own crowd. It didn't matter what you looked like, what you danced like, how old you were or anything, you just enjoyed yourself non-stop and met so many people. Nobody was paranoid. On top of that, I only ever saw five fights in four years of constant clubbing and there is a lot to say for that."

Leeroy may not have noticed how other people danced but very soon everyone was noticing how he did – his inability to pick up the popular 'rave' running steps meant his own style was unique. He had always been an athletic dancer but now he seemed to have tapped into something for which he was a natural. His sliding feet and high velocity steps offered hints of his admiration for James Brown, but there was an idiosyncratic way to his movements which was compelling. This individual style, matched with his affable nature, enormous stature and considerable presence, quickly made Leeroy a major attraction at the club, where people jostled to dance with him, and to get on his buzz.

*   *   *

"If you danced properly you'd be good."

Keith Flint was used to hearing this ambiguous compliment, and had long since given up trying to explain to on-lookers that he wasn't into dancing for technique and style, he was in it for a good time. In fact, good times were something he had been pursuing since he could remember. Despite his less than impressive school record, he was the first one amongst his friends to get a job, probably because he didn't even stick around to take the final exams – over the next few years he went through various occupations, including amongst other things investigative drilling, but nothing caught his imagination. Despite the lack of interest in his daily work, he was determined to make a go of things anyway – his lack of academic qualifications never bothered him, as he now had money in his pocket and felt like the world was his oyster: "From being one of the school's biggest hooligans I became the first to get a job and some money, so I was pretty confident of myself. I thought, 'I'm a man now and what I know at this exact minute will undoubtedly carry me for the rest of my life. What do I need to know about logorhythms for when I'm decorating the lounge?'" With a weekly pay packet coming in, Keith initially immersed himself in the so-called Casual scene, and regularly spent £60 on the right shirt for his back, whilst socialising in the Casual clubs where posing and exaggerated vanity were the norm. It was around this time that his parents split up and Keith found himself with a new step-brother, Gary, whose

The Prodigy

entrance into Keith's world had a profound effect on his development: "My brother Gary and smoking draw are the two key factors in why I turned out like I have. He wasn't into all the posing, he had much more of a hippy outlook on life, I suppose. We became great friends and he took me out on his motorbike a few times and give me a few puffs and hot knives around a few hippy's houses and I was immediately hooked." Keith's designer shorts were soon consigned to the bin, and replaced with a tiny moped on which he used to fly around town at breakneck speeds with his waist-length hair billowing out of his helmet, stopping only to puff on a joint, or to adjust the belt of his prized Paddock jacket. He started going to music festivals and to race meets like Le Mans, a lifestyle soundtracked by the music of his older peer groups, bands like Led Zeppelin, The Hamsters, Pink Floyd and Jimi Hendrix. He travelled extensively, and even spent some time working down a Cornish tin mine. These were the good times he had wanted, but all the while, despite his contentment, Keith felt a slight sense of being held back, and of having to maintain a more reserved demeanour than his ebullient nature. Whilst his friends were puffing away and chilling out, he usually wanted to get up and dance, but that was not how those people behaved. So after a while the festival lifestyle began to lose its appeal, despite the welcoming attitude of the many people he met: "It was always reggae music that I danced to the most, skanking about, and because I am quite short I found it easy to fit in because I didn't represent a threat to anyone. I was just skanking about, having a laugh, enjoying myself.

But after a while I felt limited and longed to experience something outside of my world. You've got to end up with something and you're not on this planet looking around for very long, so I wanted to experience things properly. Sleeping on the side of a Welsh mountain in a hammock, as we used to, does not make you Zen, and yet so many people think it does. If there is a Mercury Award for Zenability you don't win it just by matting your hair."

Keith sold everything he owned, gave the beloved motorbike to a close friend, and headed for the Middle East with only a small knapsack on his back. Over the next eight months, he travelled extensively through Europe, the Middle East and North Africa, and survived numerous scrapes before finally turning back for home. It was a golden era for him, but one that ended with a sharp bump when he arrived back in Essex – he was thrown out of his father's house. In the space of twenty-four hours he had gone from sleeping under the pyramids in Egypt to sleeping next to the river in Braintree.

The next day, dishevelled and fed up, he visited his good friend Ange, who promptly informed him there was a room available in the large shared house where she lived. Keith's luck seemed to be changing. He moved in the next week, settled back into life in Essex, and gradually started to go out clubbing again. Whilst he had been away, his home county had been hijacked by the rave culture, and it was not long before Keith was persuaded to sample it for himself. Despite his initial misgivings he loved it. "I thought it was the bollocks.

From the very first night I was completely hooked and had to go down there again and again. This new scene wasn't like anything I had been into before. There was a bit of a drugs scene, which made everything feel a bit more rebellious, there was more dancing than ever, and always such a good atmosphere. All the previous restrictions and shackles were thrown off me and now I could just let off. It reminded me of being a kid and your dad coming upstairs to tell you off for playing your music too loud – well, these clubs were the equivalent of never being told to turn the music down, you could do what you wanted for as long as you wanted, it was a total release. You met so many people and made loads of new friends all the time. It wasn't that you had all these blood brothers around who were ready to die for you, but there were so many friendships around at that time, that was all part of the scene. Of course, that was it for me, I was in my element. It was a fucking amazing atmosphere at those clubs."

One night at The Barn, Keith found himself dancing next to Leeroy. He had heard of Leeroy and admired his dancing before, but this was the first time he found himself right next to him. The two danced for hours and hit it off in a big way – they soon struck up a close and warm friendship. Pretty soon they were out every night at Raindance, Perception, the Astoria or any of a host of happening clubs, meeting people all the time.

For Keith this period was just one big buzz: "Leeroy was one of the local heroes and I put a few people's noses out of joint when I teamed up and became his friend. They couldn't understand how I got so much respect from him. If you danced with Leeroy down The Barn you got more of a buzz than in any other way. Leeroy was *the* biggest buzz at that club. He never used that to his advantage because if he had he wouldn't have lasted five minutes and he knew that. I was so into the scene that I wanted to find other people who'd go out everywhere, *every* night and the only person who was like that as well was Leeroy. We used to go out constantly and with him being so tall and me being so short, it was amazing, we used to just let off, we didn't give a fuck." Along with them sometimes was a girl called Sharky, whose dancing also inspired Keith: "Without a shimmer of a doubt, Sharky is one of the best buzzes of a dancer ever. It was an incredible buzz dancing with her and Leeroy. Because she was a woman it was great, not in any dirty-dancing-groin-thrusting way, but just in a way that rocked. She was flowing, we were on such a buzz people would stop and watch the three of us. I wouldn't dance like I do now if I hadn't met Sharky and perhaps even more so Leeroy. I can't say I have learnt from any other dancers, I have never been into traditional dancers and dance history. We just had a laugh, a great crew just enjoying the buzz. Those two people were a major influence on my development as a dancer. Leeroy and Sharky taught me to dance and that's the end of it."

*　*　*

It was the summer of 1989. Whilst Keith and Leeroy had been busy teaming up, Liam had also been very active. His blossoming record collection was constantly being supplemented – he now worked at a T-shirt printing factory and any spare cash he had was quickly spent on vinyl, sometimes in excess of £50 a week. When he was not at work or in a record shop, Liam was at a club, and as a result the summer passed in a blur of memorable parties, most of them at The Barn: "I just went to this club loads and got involved with this new group of people. The whole period was just a fantastic time. You would go to the club, which was always a brilliant night out, and during the course of the evening you'd hear about various all-night parties that were going down after the club had finished. Everyone was buzzing at The Barn, but that finished at 1am and everybody wanted to carry on, so it would be a convoy of thirty cars heading down to one of these parties. Even the car trips were a buzz in themselves, because it was a real communal thing. There was one place we used to go which was basically a big old house owned by this aged hippy, down this long, winding country road, which always seemed to be bathed in moonlight. You'd walk down the path on acid and it seemed to go on for miles and miles, and then suddenly you'd hear this amazing music blasting out from this house on the hill. The combination of the location, the drugs, the buzz and the music made it all so magical. It was in a small village but at three in the morning it would be packed and absolutely roadblocked. Once you got there, it was just a house with an old caravan in the back garden, but within five minutes of everyone arriving, there would be a strobe in there and this sound system booming out. I hadn't experienced anything like this feeling before. Hip-hop was about standing in the corner being bad and looking cool, but this new scene was just about being part of something."

In this celebratory atmosphere, new friendships were abundant, and it was at one of these outdoor parties that Liam first talked to Keith. The weather had been beautiful all day and held right through the night, so the whole crowd stayed on to watch the sunrise. Liam was DJ-ing inside the Transit van, when a scruffy, long-haired figure in a sheepskin Afghan body warmer and army regulation greens walked up to the side of his deck and said, "I love the tunes you are playing man, you're rocking, drop us something really funky." Liam duly obliged and in the process made himself a new friend. "Everyone knew Leeroy and Keith just because they were these two punters who danced so well. The vibe was always wherever they were dancing. Keith was a real hippy, he had been travelling and I had heard all about him and what he got up to, because everyone's faces were familiar at these clubs. I played him these funky tunes and then watched him dancing next to the van in all this weird gear, with the camp fire in the background and all these people around having an amazing time. We got to know each other from then on, but only really as faces to acknowledge, not great mates or anything."

In fact, Keith was so impressed with Liam's DJ-ing that before the night was finally over he asked him if he would mix a tape for him to play at home. A few days later, Keith was on his way round to Leeroy's when Liam pulled his car up alongside the pavement and wound down the window. "Here's that tape I promised you." Liam made to drive off, but remembered something and said, "Oh, by the way, I've put a few of my own tracks on the other side, see what you think." Keith put the tape into his sheepskin coat and promptly forgot about it. Leeroy was waiting for him when he arrived so they headed straight for Raindance, one of the country's best parties. It was a superb night, and they returned home in high spirits – it was only when Leeroy went to switch on the stereo that Keith remembered the tape in his pocket that Liam had given to him. Rather than play the established tracks he already knew, Keith flipped the tape over to listen to Liam's own work, noticing as he did the name of a keyboard model scribbled on the cassette, which appeared to be Liam's band moniker – The Prodigy.

The impact of that tape was, in short, unbelievable. Keith and Leeroy danced around the room to the immense tunes that were thumping out of the stereo – they couldn't believe that this was the work of the quiet DJ from down The Barn. Various dance moves instantly sprang to mind as the two played the tape over and over again, suggesting moves to each other and getting off on the music, as Leeroy adroitly remembers: "We were buzzing our tits off."

Such was the impression the tape made that the two friends resolved to speak to Liam the next time they saw him, to ask if they could dance alongside him whilst he played those tunes – the opportunity to get that much buzz with such good music was one they could not resist. Sure enough, a week later, Liam was spotted at The Barn and Leeroy and Keith timidly approached him, a nervous facade that hid their usual energetic buoyancy. Despite

Liam's obvious shyness, the three agreed that it would be great to get something going. Liam had wanted to do so for some time, but would never have gone onstage alone; Leeroy and Keith equally wanted to get up and buzz to this music, but they needed Liam's tunes. So it was loosely agreed that the trio would start an act, which was to also include Keith's friend Sharky. Liam however, was still uncomfortable with the idea of just him and dancers onstage, and was convinced that they needed more elements to make the act dynamic and viable. He settled on the idea of an MC, but at this stage he knew of no-one who could do the job.

Keith however knew a friend called Ziggy, who had a black book of contacts as big as they come, and after suggesting this to Liam, The Prodigy agreed to take him on board as their manager. Ziggy's entrance into the fray was well-timed for two key reasons. Firstly, he knew dozens of promoters and within days had booked the band's first ever PA at a club called The Labyrinth in Dalston.

Secondly, he put forward the name of an MC who just might be able to do the job – Maxim Reality. Ziggy remembered how one night he and Maxim had been out watching a show by America's Mr. Lee, when they had both got up onstage with the band and Maxim had seemed to be more adept at MC-ing than the headline act himself. Maybe this could be the guy The Prodigy were looking for?

Maxim, aka Keith Palmer or Keeti, was based in Peterborough and was an active MC on the town's excellent reggae scene, a trade he had learnt from his brother and MC, Starkey Ban Tan. From his early days Maxim had written poetry and verse, and as a kid had taught himself to MC and thus found a rhythmical vehicle for his expression by chatting over the records of sound systems in the local area. Like the rest of The Prodigy, Maxim also went through the breakdancing and hip-hop phase but reggae always held the strongest fascination for him, because of the highly articulate nature of reggae MCs, as well as the beats and basslines. As a teenager he watched his brother working the local sound systems, but it wasn't until he was 17 that he made his first appearance on stage himself at a local club in Basingstoke, which broke the daytime monotony of his YTS in electronic maintenance.

Around this time he had his first taste of hip-hop and immediately liked the high lyrical articulacy and heavy beats of the form. His musical aspirations progressed a step further shortly after when he teamed up with a musician from Nottingham called Ian Sherwood, under the moniker of Maxim Reality and Sheik Yan Groove. The music was experimentalist and extremely unorthodox, an unusual mix of reggae, hip-hop and world percussion, and despite Maxim's continued preference for his reggae roots, this was a formative period for him – Sherwood was an accomplished musician and taught Maxim much about musical history, as well as introducing him to the records of a whole new spectrum of bands, such as George Clinton, Bootsy Collins, Gil Scott Heron and a plethora of blues and jazz players. Unfortunately, the pair's musical productions never attracted any serious interest from record companies, so after an enjoyable three years they went their separate ways. Maxim, like Keith, decided that he wanted to experience life outside of England, and set off around Europe and North Africa for a shorter period of three months.

It was whilst he was away travelling that Maxim realised the importance of music in his life, and so on his return to Britain he moved to London and prepared himself to break into music. In the first week of being there, he was on a battered old red bus with his cousin travelling through Dalston, when a peculiar-looking old lady approached and started talking to him. She told him that she could read palms and would he mind if she tried his? Not wanting to appear rude, Maxim somewhat nervously offered his upturned hand and sat amazed as she told him her prediction of his future – one day she could see him talking to thousands of people who would all be listening to what he had to say. It may have been a total coincidence and a trivial event, but it gave Maxim the extra confidence to pursue his goal. He threw himself into the London reggae scene and became embroiled in the music of artists such as Ninja Man, Supercat and Professor Nuts, Papa San, as well as all the MCs around on the underground reggae scene. At the same time he picked up nuances from the hip-hop realms of lyrical talents like Public Enemy and Eric B and Rakim, the result of which created in his style an unusual mix of many genres. Even so, his main experience up until this point had been in reggae, so when his friend Ziggy phoned him up and mentioned there was a 'rave' band in Essex who wanted him to MC for them, he was a little unsure of what to expect, as his minimal experience of the rave scene was mostly just bleeps, with little raw beats or heavy bass. Nevertheless, he accepted without hesitation. A week later he received a phonecall and a tape through the post from a quietly spoken guy named Liam. Suitably impressed, he made his way to The Labyrinth in Dalston for the first PA. The night of their debut show was to be the first time he had met any of The Prodigy.

CHAPTER 2

"He came in and played the stuff and I was immediately impressed – it wasn't that the music was a finished masterpiece, it was rather more that he had a good street vibe about him ... and the music had enough innovation to interest me. It is very rare that a record company is into a tape to that degree on first hearing, but we were..."

Nick Halkes of XL Records

"We've only ever had one other PA here and they were bottled offstage after two songs." With these dubious words of encouragement, The Prodigy were welcomed to their first ever PA by Joe, the owner of The Labyrinth in Dalston, a particularly rough area of north-east London. Despite not being onstage until 11pm, the band had arrived enthusiastically early at about 1 o'clock in the afternoon, and therefore had a good ten hours to sit and ponder on the owner's thinly veiled cautionary welcome. "We half-expected loads of name acts to have played there," remembers Keith, "so when Joe told us about the first group being bottled offstage we were absolutely shit scared." In the weeks leading up to the debut PA, Leeroy, Sharky and Keith had made up costumes for themselves, which consisted of green and white outfits with a large white circle emblazoned on each of their chests, and they had all played Liam's tape over and over until it was memorised, so they seemed relatively well prepared. The only snag was that they were yet to meet the fifth member of the band, their MC, Maxim.

As Maxim sat on the bus from Tottenham he wondered to himself what this evening was going to be like, and his mind wandered back to the only other 'rave' he had been to up until now. After calling a number with the pre-arranged location, he had joined his friends in a convoy to the site of the party. Once the music had started he was quite interested, and the lights were impressive enough, but the music did not really grip him. His friends all appeared to be having a great night, perhaps because they were taking E's, but as Maxim was strictly into smoking he kept away from that. After four hours, they retired to their car for a smoke and sat crammed inside, enjoying a joint. Within ten minutes there was a tap on the window, frosted by the cold chill outside. The driver wound down the opaque glass and a policeman shoved his head into the car and sarcastically greeted them, whilst a large Alsation dog growled at his side. Maxim froze and wondered what on earth was going on, and secretively dropped the joint into the footwell of the back seat. He and his friends were told to get out of the vehicle and when Maxim raised his head out of the car he was amazed to see several thousand people huddled together outside a now empty warehouse, surrounded by police and dogs with the luminous flash of the squad cars illuminating the scene in a perverse imitation of the strobes that had been whirling frantically just minutes earlier.

"This is your stop mate." Maxim was jolted back to the present by the bus driver, whereupon he quickly jumped off the bus and headed around the corner to the venue. Once inside he introduced himself to The Prodigy and spent an awkward few minutes getting to know them a little better – after all, in just four hours he would be onstage as their MC. His flutter of nerves eased when Liam, who appeared to be the quietest of the four, explained that they had loads of their friends from Braintree coming to the gig, so they should be well supported. Maxim was then shown the set list and they ran through the running order to double check that he knew all the tracks they would be playing. After donning his own costume, the band were now ready for the show.

It was a short set of eight songs but the impact was dramatic. Although the first tune was a little stunted because of nerves, The Prodigy soon began to loosen up. Leeroy and Keith had taken half an E before the show, a habit they very quickly learnt to quash, as the paranoia of being on stage in front of people matched with the paranoia of the drug itself made for a very uncomfortable night of hyperventilating, with innumerable mix-ups over who was dancing to which part and when. The show was made all the more difficult by the fact that it was totally live, using no backing tapes, with Liam firing off all the samples and playing all the music himself. Not that any of this proved to be much of a problem. By the time the PA had ended, the small crowd of 250 people were captivated – there was no repeat of the previous band's bottle attack. For Maxim, it was a strange yet exciting experience: "I just remember being put on this stage in the middle of what was a dance scene, with these four people I had only just met, and I just stood at the back with a mike in my hand chatting a couple of times. Meanwhile, the rest of the band were doing their shit and everyone was going wild, it just went off. It all happened so quickly it was weird, but really good. I thought it was wicked but I didn't really think anything more of it other than that I would like to do it again." Maxim would get his chance to play again sooner than he expected – such was the impression that the band made on the owner Joe that he immediately asked them to return in two weeks and play the Saturday night, when the club would be packed with over 1000 people. Liam consequently phoned Maxim up and asked him if he would like to become a permanent member of The Prodigy – he did not need asking twice.

In the fortnight between the debut and their next show, Liam took Maxim to one side and explained the stylistic changes that he would like to be made before then – the problem was that although Maxim had improvised very well that first night, his musical background made him too vocal, too convoluted for a dance act. Maxim listened to what Liam had to say and quickly realised the role he had to play was more subtle, more linear: "A reggae MC is a more lyrical thing, where he is appreciated for what he has to say as well as the actual rhythms and phonetics, whereas the dance scene is not like that, everyone is there to dance, they don't want to stand and listen carefully to some guy rapping away all night. I was filling the music up with too many lyrics, cluttering things up, and after talking to a few people and listening to other MCs on the scene like Hardcore General, I knew I could do that much and more, so I toned down my style. That was the style, not to say anything too deep or complex because that would have been out of context. The demands of MC-ing for The Prodigy are different, using simple words and lines that are involved in the scene, it's more subconscious. Once I had realised that simple fact, my reggae, hip-hop and jazz background proved to be a bonus rather than a hindrance, it gave me an advantage in that I had nuances and a different style from most dance MCs – I have always believed that originality is by far the most important feature for any MC."

With this small problem settled, The Prodigy were better equipped to play the numerous PAs that Ziggy had very swiftly organised for them. But before they could do that, Liam had some amazing news for the rest of the band – at the end of the next month he had record coming out. It was Christmas 1990 and Liam had been actively writing this music for only ten months.

★   ★   ★

The Prodigy

The record in question consisted of four tracks from the demo tape Liam had initially played to the fledgling band, and the record company who were to release the vinyl was XL, a highly credible subsidiary of Beggars Banquet. Although the label at this stage was still relatively young, it had already established itself as a perceptive scout for underground acts that were buzzing in the clubs. At the helm were Tim Palmer and Nick Halkes in their south London offices. XL was only the second record company Liam had approached – he had sent his new Prodigy tape of ten tunes to Tam Tam Records (who had previously worked with Cut To Kill), but they declined him outright. This dismissal did not deter Liam remotely – he sent XL a tape and followed that up with a phone call to Halkes, where he requested, and was granted, a meeting at the label's offices. The day of the meeting arrived and Liam nervously made his way to London, accompanied by a handful of friends who generously supported him. Up until now, Liam had no experience of the people he was about to meet, other than his knowledge that Palmer owned the Groove Records shop in London where Liam used to buy much of his vinyl. Palmer's mother used to work behind the counter, a lady of the age and older generation not normally associated with such left-field dance music, but they quickly realised that she was far from out of touch. On weekends, Liam and his friends would drive into town and go to Groove Records, where they would test Mrs. Palmer out, deliberately asking for the most obscure imported underground dance release they could think of, usually tracks that no-one but the most dedicated dance specialist DJ would have heard of. Time and again they would stand amazed as the lady listened to their requests, then immediately replied, "Yeah, I know the track, new in this week, check it out."

Liam recalls the meeting at XL as a fairly nervous time: "I booked a demo appointment and went in trying to relax 'cos all my friends were waiting outside, but I was shitting myself. I was in there for about an hour in this small room, and they seemed to be quite into it, but not over the top. They were the first people in the industry I had actually sat down with and played my stuff to, so I was pleased I had got that far. I came away from there thinking I wouldn't hear much more about that, as they had just said, 'We'll get back to you.'" A week later Liam was working away in the T-shirt factory when the company pay-phone rang. He picked it up and was told that XL were to offer him a singles deal with immediate effect, and could he come in as soon as possible to get started? Liam replaced the receiver, tried to control himself for a few seconds then gave up and jumped around the office, much to the bemusement of his confused colleagues. Liam couldn't believe his luck – he had only approached two record companies, and the second one had snapped him up.

That in itself is an indication of the quality of the material that Liam had presented – record companies after all, are businesses, and XL clearly thought that the young, quiet kid had something that they could sell. Nick Halkes of XL explains why they were so keen to sign Liam on to their books, and why the music he played to

The Prodigy

them stood out from the hundreds of tapes they receive every day: "During the first phonecall Liam made to me, he explained his role in the hip-hop band Cut To Kill and filled me in on his musical background, so I knew a little of what to expect when he came in. It is worth bearing in mind that we do a lot of these type of demo interviews and by far the vast majority prove to have absolutely nothing of any worth. Liam sounded relatively sussed for an unsigned act but it was really only a mild curiosity that made me book the meeting. He came in and played the stuff and I was immediately impressed – it wasn't as if he walked in the room and was a complete star type, or that the music was a finished masterpiece, it was rather more that he had a good street vibe about him, he was clearly coming from a pretty solid underground angle, and the music had enough innovation to interest me. The tape consisted of some pretty raw techno with breakbeats in there, and that was pretty fresh as a concept, the idea of using breaks and combining them with techno influences. There were a small handful of other people experimenting with a few ideas like that, but there was definitely nothing established, nothing concrete in that area, so that excited me very much. I felt there was something there with a different angle, and the breakbeat thing sounded exciting, a uniquely British perspective in a way, because the people who were making speeded up breaks were from the hip-hop community. Alongside the musical impression he made, which I have to say was pretty strong, there was always the other side to any act – as a record company you have to see an artist with vision, with a few ideas, not necessarily complete and comprehensive, but a sense of vision for what he is doing.

Now, although Liam was quiet and it was obvious that there was a hell of a lot missing from The Prodigy as a viable concern, he struck me as someone who had the degree of vision that we need in order to feel comfortable about signing a deal. It is important to bear in mind that at this stage there was no Prodigy act, it was just Liam, but there was a feeling that he could progress and develop and that he was aware of possibilities musically and otherwise. It is very rare that a record company is into a tape to that degree on first hearing, but we were, and I guess that is a tribute to Liam's music."

It was small wonder that the tape was so impressive – it was a composite of Liam's work over a period of many months, during which time he had been totally immersed in the scene, going out to clubs and raves, then returning home late to the mini-studio in his bedroom, where he started work on new material while he was still on the buzz of his night out. As such, his detailed knowledge of the scene was directly reflected in his own work. It was a prolific time, with Liam writing many new tracks every week, and constantly listening to songs such as Renegade Soundwave's 'The Phantom', Patti J's 'Right Before My Eyes' and scores of other underground acts like Meat Beat Manifesto and Joey Beltram, to name but a few. The resulting ten-track demo that started both The Prodigy as a band and as a recording artist, was a collection of pure underground tunes. The four tracks that were lifted from the demo and used for the first record were 'Android', 'Everybody in the Place', 'We're Gonna Rock' and 'What Evil Lurks', using the fourth track's name as the EP title for the February 1991 release.

The Prodigy

★   ★   ★

When Liam announced that he had a record deal, the four friends who made up the rest of The Prodigy were understandably a little surprised. Keith and Leeroy, as well as Sharky had simply wanted to get a buzz dancing to Liam's music. In fact, Keith had been all set to go travelling again, this time to Thailand, and had his tickets booked and plans made. Then his grandmother died, he had his travel money stolen, and around the same time got arrested for smoking weed in Soho Square, so circumstances seemed to frustrate his plans to leave the country. It was shortly after this run of bad luck that he heard Liam's tape. Maxim had merely accepted an invitation to MC with four complete strangers. Within a matter of weeks, they had played in front of 1000 people and released their debut vinyl on one of the premier underground dance labels. Keith had initially harboured less lofty ambitions: "All I wanted to do when we started the band was play at Raindance, which was *the* big outdoor event really. Then when the Gulf War started I was absolutely gutted, because I thought, 'Fuck me, I hope we can play at Raindance before I get conscripted. That fucking Hussein, how inconsiderate, I want to play at Raindance, you bastard."

As a debut release, the 'What Evil Lurks' EP was a satisfactory opening volley. Despite having no crossover success with the mainstream charts or media, it sold a healthy 7000 copies, which at that point was a decent chunk of records for an underground and unknown act.

In addition, it was encouragingly well-received by the specialist dance press. XL were pleased with the response to this first cautious release. Years later, when The Prodigy's success was considerably greater, the vinyl was still a regular hardcore club request, and copies have exchanged hands in collectors' circles for over £120. The music itself was excitingly fresh and very raw – a low budget production with ropey quality, but this only added to the overall raw street feel. This angle was complemented by Liam's choice of instrument – his trusty Roland W30, which unlike the ubiquitous Atari's, had a rough, unique sound all of its own. As the vast majority of his contemporaries were using technically more sophisticated equipment, this gave Liam his own sound, a nasty edge which remained with The Prodigy's records constantly. At the same time, despite its simplicity, the W30 also offered Liam the use of its own Midi system, which opened up whole new areas of sound potential. The resultant record was a ferocious burst of breakbeats and murderously tough rhythms, laden with samples (including one from *The Shadow* radio series of the 1940s – "what evil lurks in the heart of men"), eerie synth auras and melodic bass, all treated with an originality that was so often lacking in minimalist music. It was a viciously underground release, and a clear notice of intent from The Prodigy.

Alongside Liam's highly innovative and street level music, The Prodigy adopted another unique policy which was virtually unparalleled in the scene at this time – they gigged rigorously and non-stop. Over the ensuing months The Prodigy's flying start was to be consolidated with dozens of PAs across the country and even one in Italy, as their adrenalin-fuelled show, combined with the debut EP, impacted upon the scene with impressive effect. Each week saw at least three shows, sometimes as many as six, including the occasional two shows in one evening. Over this opening four-month period they succeeded in playing to tens of thousands of people – this is where The Prodigy's development differs from the major rock acts that were at equivalent stages in their careers. Whereas a fledgling rock band might feel very satisfied with an audience of 500, The Prodigy found themselves in front of crowds in excess of 5000 on many occasions, such was the massive extent of the scene at this point. They were effectively dropped into a gig circuit that only major rock acts could compete with in terms of numbers. This was not always the case though – at their fifth gig they played Hatfield College on a Wednesday night, where the crowd numbered nine in total. Five of these were the security, and the head guard himself was in fact the support act. The flyer for the night was a photocopy of a scribbled beer mat, and the crowd was so small that Keith joined them dancing on the floor, rather than spend all night onstage trying to create a hardcore vibe with four people. As a rule though, this was a busy time, filled with a series of very large PAs. One night they might play to a couple of hundred at a small East End club, then follow that with a performance in front of 10,000 at one of the many huge outdoor events that were going off around this time. It was a live baptism of fire, but one which the band relished.

Along the way there were various little landmarks

which in retrospect were signs that The Prodigy were a band in the ascendancy; at the time these small achievements were often lost in the blur of gigs and PAs that filled these hectic days. The Barn had changed management and eventually closed down, and on the final sad night the band were delighted to hear the DJ play 'Android' – considering the importance of that venue to the band's very existence, it was a particularly poignant moment. A week later, Maxim was walking through a shopping centre when he popped into W.H.Smith to buy a magazine, and as he did he noticed the Dance Chart listings, with The Prodigy's EP at No.30. As the smile broke across his face he thought to himself, "I know that guy" before remembering that he was in fact in the band himself. Another night whilst Leeroy and Keith were out on a social evening at Raindance, they suddenly heard 'Everybody In The Place' being played, and to their amazement the 12,000 people crammed into the gargantuan tent immediately recognised the track and just lifted up off the floor and heaved their way through the entire song, in a sea of moving bodies. As unknown faces in the crowd, no-one noticed the two friends standing there, watching the massive reaction and smiling broadly. This incident at Raindance signified the excellent progress that The Prodigy's deliberate and extensive gig policy had at this point – they were booked because promoters knew of their record, then when they played the show people recognised the four tracks from the EP. Even if they weren't PA-ing at a club, one or more of their tracks would invariably get played. As a result, The Prodigy were getting enormous coverage and exposure on the scene, week in, week out.

The actual live show at this point was still relatively infant, but a happy balance was beginning to develop within the band, as the practice from the rapid succession of gigs honed their act. The only downside to this period was the loss of Sharky, who left the band during this spell. After the initial buzz of the very first shows, the band began to get more and more into the idea of PAs, whilst Sharky prefered instead to go out clubbing, as they all had done before The Prodigy started. When she missed a couple of gigs and her interest seemed to subside, it became clear that it would probably be best for everyone concerned if they parted ways and The Prodigy reverted to just a four-piece. There was no acrimony involved, and Sharky and the band remain good friends to this day. Soon after The Prodigy decided that if they were to adopt a fully professional approach then they should rehearse. Thus far, they had never actually practiced, so an afternoon was arranged where they all drove to Liam's house and set up their gear. It was to be their first and last rehearsal. Away from the vibe and atmosphere of the shows, with hundreds or thousands of people dancing to their music, the band found the situation impossible. After twenty minutes of arguments and uncomfortable shufflings from Leeroy and Keith, and muted efforts from Maxim and Liam, they called it a day. Clearly, the actual PAs were where the band learnt their craft, feeding off the audience, seeing which tracks worked, which dance moves earned good reactions, a very direct and mutual experiment with the audience that was to be on-going and ever-changing. As such the band remain a uniquely interactive live act, and this failed practice session is the origin of this approach.

Another side to this professional attitude was the band's views on the use of drugs. As part of the culture of their scene, ecstasy was a constant factor in their social life before The Prodigy began. Each one of the band had indulged in, and enjoyed, the ecstasy experience, and they were aware of the strong arguments both for and against its use. Liam knew that for him it was not essential to enjoy the music, that the vibe for him was still there without it: "Let's face it, you could drop some ecstasy and go shopping and you'd enjoy that a lot more as well." Keith and Leeroy had both been arrested for smoking dope, and Keith had even been taken to court, where he sat in the courtroom trying not to smile as the hefty policeman who had accosted him in Soho Square related to the judge how he had seen the defendant "rolling a large roll-up type cigarette containing a brown sticky substance, that from my wide experience I know to be cannabis resin". They knew that unfortunately people had died from ecstasy, but they felt that the general vibe it created seemed to be far more peaceful than at clubs where alcohol was the norm. Even so, once the band's first PA was over and they had seen the effect of half a tab of E on Keith and Leeroy whilst trying to play a show, the band agreed that total abstinence was the best policy. It was a deliberate and quite calculated decision – if people came to see The Prodigy and they were incapable of performing at their very best because they had dropped an E, it was clearly an unfair presumption on the band's part. Furthermore, the band themselves soon realised that the buzz of the band and the PA itself was sufficient without any artificial help. As Liam explains: "The drugs didn't really have a great part in my enjoying the music, it was second to the music which I was so heavily into, as we all were. Yes, I experimented with acid and E but nothing else. And even before The Prodigy started I surprised myself by how sensible I was. Some of my friends were doing four or five Es a week but I never got into it that much. When we started doing lots of PAs, the drugs side totally calmed down. We decided that in order to be more professional onstage it had to stop. When you are on E, you are open to so many feelings and emotions, you just couldn't handle drugs onstage. So that was that, we stopped there and then. We are always off the E's when on stage. It slowly calmed down and within six months I had stopped taking Es altogether."

All the time The Prodigy began making these concessions to professionalism, they were playing more and more shows, between which the band would often meet round Liam's house and listen to the masses of new material he had written. "The buzz of the band took over from The Barn and we treated the band as our night out, so we would be in the crowd dancing after the show most nights. Then I would go home and write, and the type of music I was coming out with fitted perfectly into what the scene was about, it was all very closely linked at that point." The band had to learn the new songs through track previews at his house or just by mailed tapes – either way, the first time they ever performed a new track was always at an actual PA. On several occasions, when time prevented tracks being previewed in advance, the first time they had even heard a particular track was when they found themselves dancing to it during a show. Similarly, the dance moves were all improvised and spontaneous, with no preparatory choreographing or ideas, which was also a policy that Maxim followed with his free-form MC style. In this fashion, The Prodigy ensured that each gig was different. The policy paid off – shortly after their tenth gig, Ziggy had informed them that they had been booked to play Beckton's Raindance the next week. For all of the band this was the biggest success so far. After all, Raindance was *the* major show and one that they had all wanted to play (Saddam Hussein permitting). So only ten shows after they played their first ever PA to 250 people in Dalston, they were playing in front of 10,000 heaving bodies at Raindance.

Another of these early shows was at the club Telepathy in Bow, east London, an underground warehouse of the most spartan kind. On that particular night, it was pouring down with torrential rain and Keith turned up with a brutal case of 'flu, but much to the band's surprise he refused to consider not going onstage, despite having to lie down every five minutes before the show had even started. In the soundcheck, the beleaguered Keith was standing next to the DJ leaning on his deck when he heard this amazing tune coming out from the speakers, something harder than anything Keith had heard before. He turned to the DJ and said, "This tune is the bollocks mate, who's this?" and to his surprise the DJ said, "I don't know, it's your mate playing it." Keith looked up and there was Liam soundchecking a new tune. Parts of the track sounded familiar and finally Keith realised it was a radical re-mix of a tune they had been playing since their very first PA, a track called 'Charly'. Suitably buoyed by this immense new tune, Keith felt much better prepared for the show itself. When they went onstage, there was rain pouring through the ceiling on to the stage boards, but this was how the band liked it, underground in the extreme. Despite his admirable enthusiasm, two songs into the set Keith was deathly white, and throughout the set he was so ill that during his break he had to lie down to avoid vomiting. By the middle of the show his head was spinning and his vision severely blurred, and when The Prodigy finally finished, he was violently sick backstage. He spent the journey home lying down in the back of the van, with the tune to 'Charly' ringing through his aching, swirling head.

CHAPTER 3

"We wanted to make the music, not the money. The record was out, if you like it, buy it, if you don't, then don't."

Liam

"One thing that led us to believe we were on to something potentially big was the fact we were getting phone calls from record shops and pirate radio stations asking for 'Charly' before we had even mastered it. We hadn't even cut or promo-ed the record, but off the back of the band's live following and the sheer number of PAs The Prodigy had played, we were being asked for the record. That is very rare, very unusual, in fact probably unique in my experience." Nick Halkes at XL was not alone in being taken aback by the volume of interest that was building around The Prodigy's second single 'Charly' months before it was even released. By March of 1991 the band were immersed in a hectic live schedule across the whole country, and all this time Charly was a permanent feature of their set and one which was a guaranteed floor filler – between March and the record's August release date over 50,000 people would hear the track at various huge outdoor events nationwide. With the recognition that 'What Evil Lurks' produced, combined with the heady anticipation for the next single, it appeared that The Prodigy might even break the national charts. As it turned out, the record's massive commercial success was, by the time of its eventual release, almost unstoppable.

The lead tune on the four-track EP was in fact written before Christmas of the previous year, after yet another post-party writing session. The particular evening in question, Liam came home, switched on the television and was confronted by the weird, almost surreal children's information advert featuring a bizarre tortoise-shell coloured animation cat with his own dialect and interpreting infant chum. "I thought it was so hilarious, it was the bollocks. I thought if I put that to a really hard sound it would be something totally new." The only problem was that being an advert, Liam did not know when it would be shown again; fortunately, the clip was between two halves of a 1970s kids programme called *Double Decker*, so Liam tuned in the next week and sure enough, the weird advert came up again. With the required sample under his belt, Liam was now free to put his idea into action: "I took those sounds and put them on to this really hard back beat. The first mix was done at the very end of 1990, and was played at our first PA at

The Labyrinth, but I eventually re-mixed it again for the single. That second mix was basically more techno, more danceable and more listenable if you like, whereas the original had a really heavy ragga sub-bass line running through it." This second mix was the version that had so excited Keith at Telepathy that night, and pretty soon the reaction from the band's followers was equally enthusiastic. When the song was released on promo, all the major underground DJs were playing it most nights, and there was a tangible and very sizeable swell of underground support for the track once XL had started their promotions. Expectations for the release began to verge on the feverish.

The lead track was a crunching manic offering with a rumbling bass running throughout a clanking, fast and frenzied bruiser of a tune. The weird samples leant the track an eerie twist, with the line "Charly says never go out without telling your mummy first" punctuating what was otherwise a very hard release. The occasional scat singing further emphasised the atmosphere of a world beyond weird. In the context of its time, it was a hard and innovative track. As with all Prodigy records, Liam had endeavoured to put out four substantial underground -oriented cuts, rather than letting the lead tune carry three other weaker pieces. "The samples definitely helped the track take off, but because I didn't want it to be seen as a novelty record I made sure that the tracks on the flip side were radically different." With the EP this was especially the case, and 'Your Love' in many senses won the band more respect and interest than 'Charly' did, with its piano intro and fuzzy atmospheres, hectic noises and frantic pace, all making for a melting pot of sounds with a more uplifting feel than 'Charly' itself.

It was a strong release and XL were understandably excited about its potential, but nevertheless maintained their cautious initial goal of putting out a hard underground track for the scene. Any mainstream crossover success at this stage would be seen as a bonus. Once the record was out on the shop shelves, nobody could have imagined what was about to happen next. In short, 'Charly' was a massive commercial smash. The record reached No.3 in the national charts, No.1 in the nationwide Dance Charts, and won the band's spartan, low budget dance video generous television exposure on *Top of the Pops* (the band refused to appear on the show live) as well as *The Chart Show*. One month after its release the band played their biggest PA yet, in front of 30,000 people at Perception. The track was included in a media Top 5 of tracks that best represented 1991, and eventually went on to sell in excess of 200,000 copies in the UK alone. Against his father's advice, Liam finally gave up his day job.

Almost overnight, it appeared to many that The Prodigy had gone from a relatively unknown act to huge cult status and massive record sales. A clue to this success is in the media reviews of the track, which invariably precluded their assessment of 'Charly' with "you know the one". *Everyone* did indeed know 'Charly' and at the centre of the scene, that 'everyone' represented a sizeable record-buying public. The track captured the imagination of the underground, whilst the infectious and recognisable sample won enormous crossover

The Prodigy's first ever press shot, December 1990.

Clockwise: Mike Champion, Gary (Lighting), Ziggy, Sharky.

Old school Keith, 1989

Sharky, live on stage, 1991.

The Prodigy, 1991.

Liam and Maxim late on stage as usual.

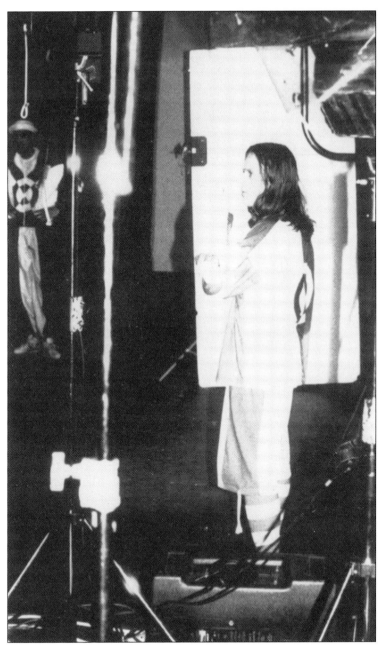

Keith during the video shoot for 'Charly'.

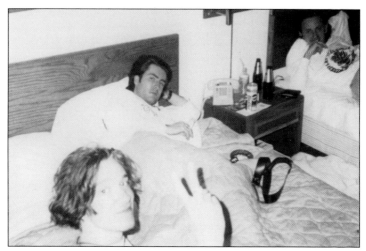

Liam at the XL office with A&R men
Nik Hawkes and Richard Russell

Filming the 'Everybody In The Place' video in New York.

Maxim, late 1991.

Laguna Beach, 1991.

Maxim and Liam, live at Amnesia, 1992.

success. In addition the band's continued live work cemented the impact. It was a powerful package.

Even so, Liam was still surprised by the degree of success, maybe because he had not considered mainstream progress as an element of the band's environment: "When it charted I was totally shocked, and we didn't really know what to make of it because this was something that we had never looked for. It meant more to us to play a big rave in front of 10,000 people than to chart with a single. Live, you can see the reaction for yourself, the feedback is instant, but a chart single is different. It's good, but not as amazing as a great PA."

At this point, it is worth placing The Prodigy's enormous success with 'Charly' into some degree of context within their own scene. Before 'Charly' was released, N Joi was arguably the biggest act around, but their two key hits did not achieve the same level of commercial success as The Prodigy's second single, and they never fully fulfilled the massive potential they had threatened at one stage. Similarly, Shades of Rhythm were a higher profile act than The Prodigy, and had also enjoyed a modest level of success. Cubik 22 and T99 had enjoyed some limited chart recognition, as had Adamski, and there were bands such as Altern 8, Dream Frequency and 808 State all furthering the cause as well. The key however, was that only a handful of these acts had a substantial live show. The Prodigy were all fans and admirers of N Joi and Shades of Rhythm and reflections of this could initially be seen in their own show, but other than that there was a noticeable dearth in live talent from the scene. The culture of shows was very much based

The Prodigy

around DAT, but that did not predispose acts to live work. The Prodigy were one of the youngest acts of all in the scene, and yet 'Charly' was bigger than any contemporary release at this point. Liam remains a little reluctant to pinpoint the reasons for this success, but his insight offers an interesting view of the scene as it was from the inside: "There were lots of successful records from the rave scene, good hard underground tunes, but none as big as 'Charly' and there are various reasons for that. Firstly, the cat sample drew a lot of people towards us that weren't really involved in the scene and yes, that new fan-base boosted its success; however, almost immediately we wondered if we had made a wrong move, but ultimately we knew we were true to ourselves and to the scene. Secondly, the rave scene was so big at that point, you could play in the underground, release a record and chart with it, because so many people were already into it. Thirdly, our musical peers seemed to fall away. Altern 8 were there but it was all samples of other people's music and I felt I had more to offer than that. Shades of Rhythm were quite big, more commercial sounding than we were, with a full vocal all the way through. N-Joi were the veterans of live techno really. Musically I took no influence from them, but visually they influenced us a little I guess. Having said all that, it is very difficult to spot why we were the most successful act, I wish I knew. I guess it was the combination of the image and visual presentation, along with the dancing and the music, which as a composite seemed to fit in with exactly what was happening at that point."

* * *

One important development which facilitated the band's sustained progress around this time was their involvement with a new manager. Much as they all loved Ziggy, it was clear that the level they had been catapulted to with the success of 'Charly' needed someone with a little more experience. Therefore, the band approached Mike Champion, then manager of the scene's leading act, N Joi, for some advice. He gave them some guest passes for an N Joi show and said he would speak to them in more length on that night. The band headed off to the show in Leyton, East London, and went to the guest door to get in. To their bemusement, when they said, "We're with N Joi" the security guard mistook them for the actual band and consequently rushed them through to the changing rooms. Once in there, they could see Mike Champion heading their way, and so they hastily dropped the spliffs they were smoking. Mike was, after all, a big name in the scene to The Prodigy, and they were not sure how to take him, or for that matter, how he would take them. They nervously stood and talked to Mike and after a brief discussion about potential management, during which time he appeared to be nothing like the ogre they had imagined, he offered to manage them himself. The deal was cemented after Mike came to a Prodigy show at Wonderland, where the band's nervous but successful PA convinced him of his intuitive feeling that this was true quality.

Mike had previously run his own shipping company, but when his brother formed the band N Joi he gave all that up and decided to manage them, much to the amazement of his friends and colleagues. Over the next two years, N Joi achieved a number of massive club hits, including the legendary 'Anthem' and 'Adrenalin', and their live show was justifiably revered. By the time The Prodigy approached Mike, N Joi were established as the premier act on the circuit. Mike was also in a partnership with another man, Mike Barnet, who true to his name was originally a hairdresser. Soon after their initial meeting the two partners went their separate ways, so that Mike Champion was left as the sole manager of The Prodigy. The decision to stop working with the successful N Joi and start managing the relativity unknown Prodigy was quite easy for Mike : "The music was well written, street level and underground. There was plenty of innovation in there, and I believe it was ahead of its time, I still do. Plus, Liam was not averse to sticking by his very strong principles and I could see that that would eventually come across very powerfully in his music. Around the same time, N Joi started to slow up and become inactive, and there were a couple of managerial difficulties, so all in all it was an easy decision to take."

The effect of Mike's involvement in the band was substantial and immediate. He knew hundreds of contacts in the scene and quickly re-negotiated a stronger deal with XL. The Prodigy's PAs were now arranged meticulously, and the band took on their first road manager, lighting man and crew. With this increasing professionalism the band began to take themselves and their responsibilities in terms of entertaining people more seriously, and the whole circus moved up several gears, including an increase in the number of PAs yet again. At the same time, they maintained their underground distaste for the increased celebrity that comes with any band's success. They still funnelled all their earnings straight back into the band for example, despite Liam being the only one to use the expensive equipment that was needed for the band's music. They also designed and funded the band T-shirts and merchandise that were becoming increasingly popular. In so doing, they could maintain maximum artistic control and input whilst meeting the increasing demands of their growing profile, without compromising their anti-star attitude.

One result of this increased professionalism was the band's first dates in the dance haven of Germany, where the audiences were left somewhat bemused by The Prodigy. Traditionally, the Teutonic market was more predisposed to basic house beats or industrial material, and the legacy of experimentalists such as Kraftwerk still hung heavily over the country, so the peculiarly English taste to The Prodigy seemed a little unpalatable to some. However, the shows were all sold out and marked an impressive start to the band's exploration of markets outside the UK.

* * *

The Limelight Club in New York was a far cry from The Barn in Braintree. It was an converted old Church complete with original stained glass windows and ecclesiastical decor, mixed with the Big Apple's very own style of underground night life. Rooms off the main areas were set aside for various activities, and every walk of life was welcomed and at home, including transvestites, gays, transexuals, lesbians, heterosexuals, bondage lovers, MPs, all of every race and creed. Go-go dancers scantily clad in skimpy underwear cavorted in cages on raised pedestals as human sideshows, whilst men wearing suits, jackets and ties with stilettos, suspenders and stockings talked idly below, fiddling with their innumerable body pierces. Liberality was the order of the day and the general atmosphere was one of 'anything goes'.

It was here that The Prodigy came for a show whilst on a short trip to film the video for their third single 'Everybody In The Place.' The day before the actual Limelight show the band were offered free tickets to Guns N' Roses at Madison Square Gardens and a private and exclusive party launching Prince's *Diamonds and Pearls* album, but with indifference that would be regretted within hours, they declined, saying they were too tired. Thankfully things got a little more lively once they were at The Limelight – the gig was well-received, even though the act and their music were relatively unknown in America. After the show, Maxim took a particular shine to one of the many high percentage cocktails on offer, and proceeded to get mind-numbingly drunk on glasses of 'Sex On The Beach', slumped against the bar, drinking through a three-foot straw. When Mike came over to see how he was, Maxim was just ordering yet another drink from the heavily made-up and rather hefty barmaid, who unbeknown to the MC was in fact a six-foot Texan man. Mike, who was perhaps a little more in control of his faculties, watched in horror as Maxim took the drink from the barmaid, paused, tilted his head to one side and said, "You've got mighty large wrists for a woman."

Shortly afterwards, there was a gun shot outside and the band flew under the tables, whilst the regulars carried on drinking and chatting as if nothing had happened. Only after ten minutes under the table did Keith finally poke his head out cautiously and say, "Was that a real gun shot then?" He got up, brushed himself down and ventured into the toilet to relieve himself, and fumbled with the zip of his stage gear, which at this point consisted of shiny black PVC shorts, covered in zips and with chains running from his neck down to under his crutch. As he did so, he looked around and saw a motley crew of people, all dressed in similar garb (only this was their normal evening wear), looking and leering with decided relish at this fresh-faced young Englishman who appeared to be heavily into bondage. Keith bolted out the door and into the changing room, where he pissed into an empty bottle, before throwing it out of the window, all the time mumbling to himself, "I'm having none of that."

The video for 'Everybody In The Place' was shot on location in and around New York, and the band even convinced some workmen to let them film in a semi-demolished building, only to have their hopes dashed with problems over safety permits. Still, the film was a fast-moving dance video that featured all of the band in a collage of split-second clips, essentially a pure dance video, but one that at this stage suited the band's image well. Dance as a medium, especially that with little or no vocals, is much harder to video effectively without a lead vocalist to focus on at length, and with the band's limited public persona this was an ideal compromise.

The record however, was not compromising in the slightest. Taken from the B-side of the band's first EP, the new version of 'Everybody In The Place' was a seriously hardcore release. Once again the band thumped out a high rate of beats at a frantic pace, with a wheezing calliope-tinkled melody. On the flip side there was the thrashing hip-house of 'Rip Up The Sound System' and the excellent 'Crazy Man'. The fourth track, 'G Force' was written initially just to try out the sounds on Liam's new U220 Roland sound module – with its surging staccato rhythms it was ironically one of the strongest tracks included (this was during a period when Liam was buying old analogue synths in order to pursue the originality of sound that his old W30 had offered him when he started). The resulting commercial impact of 'Everybody In The Place' was enormous – this time the record went one better than 'Charly' and reached No. 2 (being kept off the top spot only by the re-released 'Bohemian Rhapsody') and eventually sold over a quarter of a million copies, a welcome Christmas present indeed.

Once again the band refused *Top of the Pops*, and once again the record achieved its massive popularity with almost negligible radio play. Nick Halkes at XL now began to see some of the vision that he had sensed in Liam at their very first meeting, especially with regard to their view of commerciality: "One of the unique aspects of The Prodigy that was interesting to observe was their attitude to *Top of the Pops*. It definitely showed me they had a certain integrity in terms of their vision that I had to respect, and also that Liam had a great deal of respect for the other members of the band and their views. With 'Everbody in the Place' it seemed at one point that had they done a live *Top of the Pops* it probably would have given them a No.1 record. I said "Think deeply about this. I hope in the future that you will have No.1 records your way, but bear in mind that not many people ever get the chance of a shot at No.1, let alone actually achieve it." They listened to what I had to say carefully, but their minds were firm, there was never any question of them doing it. From a label perspective it was a little disappointing but I had to respect them for that quite impressive approach."

This attitude is indicative of the underground ethos which The Prodigy carry with them at all times, and it is this tenet of anti-stardom that is quintessential to understanding the band's motivations and principles. When they turned down *Top of the Pops* for 'Charly', many people outside of their circle thought the young band were foolish and arrogant for refusing what was potentially the highlight of their musical careers. Yet the band had already decided that mass exposure and the pop media were to be avoided quite deliberately. They felt the temporary benefits of this fickle media circus were far outweighed by the damaging long-term effects. The success of 'Charly' had proven that underground promotions, respect from DJs and gruelling PA schedules were far more valuable and indeed effective in the scene than any amount of exposure on television or radio. When 'Everybody In The Place' enjoyed similar success, the possibility of joining the mainstream media conveyor belt never surfaced, and Liam maintains it was never a dilemma or contentious issue: "We said 'no' to *Top of the Pops* straight away, we desperately wanted to avoid any of that commercial angle. We wanted to make the music, not the money. The record was out, if you like it, buy it, if you don't, then don't. Too many dance bands fall into that trap which destroys them, because their success is not based on a solid foundation of underground hardcore support. I can't stress how much we were into this anti-commercial philosophy right from the start – it would have been so easy for us to have slipped into that trap but we would have none of that. I have surprised myself how much we held onto that, and it has been a crucial factor in the band's welfare – the very last thing we wanted was for The Prodigy to be a one-hit wonder. Besides, why should we go on telly so some pompous wanker can say, 'Yes, I really liked the words to that one.' We never saw ourselves as stars and that is maybe one reason why we appeal because we look like people in the crowd who have jumped up on stage. Basically the scene has no room for stars in the way guitar music or other music has. We knew that because we were so clued up about the scene ourselves. So *Top of the Pops* and other shows like it were never a possibility."

The only blemish on the band's progress at this stage was a hint of a backlash from certain magazines. Reviewing 'Everybody In The Place' *Mixmag* said, "It isn't techno because the real stuff is cleverly put together. It's not underground unless you take my advice and bury it. It's definitely not sophisticated – this is a record made for children by children. There is no love of music involved at all, just a 'let's knock it out' attitude that sucks. This is most definitely a throw away record." Liam also experienced his first taste of tabloid invention, when *The Sun* ran a piece under the headline 'Dad's the Way to Live Liam', wherein Liam allegedly espoused the virtues of living "with me old man" despite his status as a "top raver". Clearly, the tabloids had their finger on the pulse once again.

★　　★　　★

The Prodigy were not to release another single until September 1992, a lengthy public sabbatical during which time they toured extensively around Britain and Europe, as well as a small visit to America. With 'Everybody In The Place' still in the charts, they headed off on a mammoth series of PAs once more, not a strict tour as such, but still a string of continual shows. The spring 1992 American mini-tour was not intended as a promotional effort for any records, as they were yet to sign a deal in that territory, but Mike Champion booked them independently as a cautious initial foray into that massive market, including dates in Miami, San Diego, New York and Los Angeles.

Further progress was made in America when The Prodigy were signed to the legendary American label Elektra, home to The Doors amongst others. Their UK talent scout Harvey Eagle had seen the band on one of their many PAs around the country, and was convinced that given the right marketing they could have substantial success in the States. So The Prodigy joined Altern 8 as the leading proponents of a batch of groups who signed lucrative American deals in this period. Furthermore, Liam's growing reputation as a serious songwriter was reflected in requests for his re-mix skills by both The Art of Noise and Dream Frequency. The finished mixes were very warmly received by the media and underground, and raised a few eyebrows in more cynical quarters. The Art of Noise track was re-mixed to such an extent that it virtually became a Prodigy track, and was arguably the strongest piece on the *Fon Mixes* album, which also contained work by the likes of 808 State, LFO, Youth and Carl Cox. Shortly afterwards, a licensing deal was signed with Sony in Australia which capped what was a very successful period for the band. All seemed remarkably well.

That was until the band read the front cover feature in the August 1992 issue of *Mixmag* entitled 'Did 'Charly' kill rave?' Thus far, the band's ascendancy had been relatively unfettered, with two Top 5 singles, scores of sell out PAs and widespread acclaim. Inevitably, there comes a time when progress is not so easy or welcome, and during this period of vinyl inactivity The Prodigy faced their first major obstacle, when this article posed a very serious threat to their entire credibility. The piece opened with a series of personal digs at Keith, which were to continue throughout. The journalist claimed that Liam's massive single success with 'Charly' introduced the whole wave of kiddy samples that swept the country in the middle of 1992 and did much to discredit rave as a powerful subculture. The article stated – not without some credibility – that chart success for a series of amateur 'rave' versions of various kids programmes theme tunes had reduced an important subculture into a laughing stock. Shaft's 'Roobarb and Custard', Urban Hype's 'Trip to Trumpton', and the Smarties 'Sesame's Treet' were perhaps the worst offenders of this so-called teen or kindergarten rave. However, the journalist talked of The Prodigy as "the ultimate cheesy teen rave act, the epitome of rave, overground, Essex style, who make simple obvious and always over the top rave tunes." The piece went on to say, "Why do people dislike them so much? Because rave is dead and they killed it, that's why. The kick in the face that put rave permanently on the pavement came from 'Charly'." Furthermore, it described band arguments and generally derided their intelligence and musical integrity, making only the odd concession to their success. Perhaps worst of all was the photo of Liam with a gun to his head for the front cover, a photo which indirectly insinuated that The Prodigy endorsed the article's views.

The Prodigy went ballistic when they read this piece, and heated phone calls were made to the *Mixmag* office, but the temporary damage was already done. The Prodigy had been placed unwittingly in the dock and Liam, unbeknown to himself, had fired his own executioner's bullet. It was a difficult time for the band. After the initial anger and disappointment had died down however, it became clear that the article actually served as the best possible defence for The Prodigy and they suffered no long-term damage as a result of the piece. There were several omissions in the article which exposed its flawed subjectivity. There was no mention of the responsibility for rave's decline on the scene's own greed, or rather the outsiders who siphoned off the financial rewards and bled the scene dry; no mention either of the growing adulteration of ecstasy with other amphetamines and dangerously impure additives, which suddenly plunged anyone indulging at a party into a narcotic Russian roulette. There was no mention of snob DJs who helped to strangle the creativity in the scene by insisting on playing only the rarest and most obscure of dub plates in the petty battle for the dance floor elitism stakes. There was no mention of the concerted mainstream media policy of besmirching rave and its followers. No mention either of the contextual truth, in other words, the fact that 'Charly' came eighteen months before many of these poor imitations finally decided to make their dash for cash – The Prodigy had simply suffered from the copycat mentality that tarnishes much of British dance music. No mention of *Mixmag*'s derisive review of 'Everybody In The Place' some months previous. There was mention, however, of 'progressive house' a genre that *Mixmag* was currently championing; by contrast, magazines had no control over rave, it was a monster that grew without their assistance and help.

Yes, rave *was* arguably the most powerful youth movement for a decade, and yes, it degenerated into novelty cartoon samples with questionable progress being made from its very existence. But 'Charly' and The Prodigy were not the cause of that.

Mixmag has its views to which they are entitled, and this is an authorised Prodigy biography, so it could be argued that objectivity might be at a premium. It is interesting therefore to turn to one of the leading lights of the underground scene at this point, for further insight into this controversy. Dan Donnelly of Suburban Base Records, originally based in Romford, is someone who made his indifference to many Prodigy tracks well known, and he is perhaps least likely to offer support, but his objections to the *Mixmag* piece were more deep rooted than some unusual allegiance to The Prodigy. Of the whole accusation that 'Charly' was responsible for taking the scene into the mainstream, Donnelly is quite adamant: "I don't think that it was entirely responsible for taking the whole scene overground, the scene was going that way anyway and 'Charly' wasn't the only track that crossed over. It's strange the way the media picked up on that track and tried to lay the blame at their feet, and I don't think there was any one specific tune that did that. 'Charly' was a good track and it was totally unfair to do that to Liam. It wasn't just The Prodigy that the media did that to though, it was the whole rave scene, they were bored of rave and wanted to get the next thing in so they tried to force rave out – *Mixmag* tried to introduce the progressive house thing and that never really got going. At that stage, they would level any insult that they could at the rave scene, and Liam was the target of one of those insults." Perhaps more surprising is Donnelly's appraisal of the effects of this piece on The Prodigy's welfare: "I think if anything The Prodigy won more respect for that, they certainly didn't lose any amongst the underground.

The Prodigy

My label, Suburban Base, withdrew all our advertising from the magazine as a protest, not so much to defend just The Prodigy, but moreover the whole scene. Their overall criticisms of the rave scene were just not on and to pinpoint one particular act was really out of order. As far as I am concerned I don't look at The Prodigy and think they have done anything wrong and sold out or anything like that. At that point in time they were already heading that way and becoming a mainstream artist, and I don't mean that in a rude way – some people see that as a criticism, but I don't, there's nothing wrong with that. I didn't disrespect them at any time and I don't think most people in the scene did either. Most people were angered by it, not necessarily because they felt passionately for The Prodigy but because of what they saw the media was trying to do to the rave scene."

CHAPTER 4

"Three gigs a week for nine months, it was crazy, we were really buzzing. We were all still gobsmacked that we were going abroad and being in the band full-time – I still considered myself not to be working. It was a really hectic time – I could have had a baby in that time, but I barely had chance to wash my pants."

Keith

As Liam walks up to the burning camp fire, he pulls from his pocket a copy of *Mixmag* with his own face on the front cover and tosses it into the flames, standing a few seconds to make sure the paper has caught and been fully incinerated. So ends The Prodigy's video for their next single release, 'Fire', shot on a Welsh mountainside. With this track, and their subsequent debut album release, The Prodigy finally extinguished the controversy surrounding the 'rave killer' accusations, so that by the end of the year the whole sorry episode was indeed no more than a few dying embers.

The idea for the 'Fire' video was not the most revolutionary one, being simply to film the band around a camp fire, whilst entering into each of their heads to observe what was going on inside their psyche. Simple maybe, but certainly a lot safer than Keith's original suggestion of setting himself alight for three minutes. The video shoot soon degenerated into their worst yet, with constant clashes between the film crew and the tired and demotivated band. The weather was icy cold, the location on a mountainside offered no respite from the biting wind, and the provisions consisted of a sausage roll each, with plastic cups of tepid coffee every two hours. Filming did not even start until 2am, by which time the crew were displaying a miserable but perhaps understandable indifference, mumbling about unpaid overtime, whilst the band were more interested in when they could get some sleep. Leeroy in particular was not impressed with the preparations – he had suspected they were not exactly on the ball when he noticed the centrepiece fire was constructed of large planks of 4-by-2 wood, not something that is found in natural abundance amongst the heather in a Welsh valley. Matters did not improve after snatching three restless hours sleep in the van before defrosting enough to finish filming with the sunrise in the background. The band were even more disappointed when they saw the finished promotional video – the cost had been relatively high, their most expensive by a long way thus far, but the 'sophisticated computer graphics' actually looked to many observers like a reject from a 1960s B-movie. It was easily the worst video they had done.

Fortunately, the track 'Fire' was strong enough to carry itself without a classic video. The core sample resurrected the 1968 hit of the same name, a classic novelty chart topper by The Crazy World of Arthur Brown, a zany character who, amongst other things, was not averse to sporting a flaming colander on his head. Rumours in the underground that Liam had been tampering with more trancey textures were soon dispelled when this track was heard. It was harder than The Prodigy's normal offerings, with snippets of piano, an emphatic beat, and a deep bassline with a touch of ragga, which reflected Liam's (and for that matter the scene's) current interest in the dub sphere of music. Liam himself said at the time that, "it's a smokin' song instead of an ecstasy-feel rave song. It's got a reggae feel to it, because I want to link it up to the whole smoking vibe, 'cos at the end of the day everyone who goes out raving puffs." It was a hellish piece of techno, and confirmed for those doubters that The Prodigy had most definitely not sold out or softened up for the charts. On the flip side the choice was harder and better – 'Horns Of Jericho' was a serious breakbeat track with a heavy demonic jungle feel. The heralding horns and intense, quirky percussion injected the track with an individuality, and marked The Prodigy's most eerie, and probably their best, track to date. Underground DJs such as Carl Cox, Fabio and Ray Keith all played the EP and anticipation for its release was high. With the Genocide II remix of 'Horns Of Jericho' also attracting much interest, it was a strong record. This was a crucial release for the band, coming shortly after the 'rave exterminator' accusations, but The Prodigy managed to defy their critics and produce a quality EP.

The vinyl was released for only two weeks before being deleted, a policy aimed at priming the market for the forthcoming album release – the single reached No.11, but in retrospect could have done better without the limited shelf-life. By the time of the release, the band were heading towards the tail-end of their most hectic schedule of live shows thus far, with the preceding nine months being a blur of PAs (unfortunately their schedules were so tight that Liam had to turn down a remix for Take That). The scene itself enjoyed highs and lows during the summer of 1992, with commercialisation producing the dreadfully cheap imitations that caused so much damage, in contrast to a batch of the best parties, both indoors and out. The band find it difficult to even remember the dates they played – they were on a rollercoaster ride that was sweeping them ever onward, at such high speed that they had little or no time to look back, and certainly no chance of getting off. Keith probably best sums up this feeling when he describes the summer's blur of events: "Three gigs a week for nine months, it was crazy, we were really buzzing. We were all still gobsmacked that we were going abroad and being in the band full-time – I still considered myself not to be working. It was a really hectic time – I could have had a baby in that time but I barely had chance to wash my pants."

The effect of the prolific touring at this stage was

crucial – with various debates flying around about the relative merits of dance acts and the scene snobs sharpening their daggers for any sign that The Prodigy were 'selling out' in their eyes, this proliferation of shows cemented the band's growing reputation as a quality live act. Snide remarks about 'real music' that beleaguered all the bands in this genre were difficult to sustain in the face of a continued onslaught of gigs. Moreover, with the original rave scene possibly on its last legs, it was important that The Prodigy showed they were a band with their own identity, separate from that scene, and no longer reliant upon it. Three shows in particular during this period confirmed the band's capacity to survive independent of any scene: one within the scene itself at XL's massive August party, and the other two at Sound City 1992 in Sheffield and Liverpool University, both outside of the underground scene.

The XL Vision show was a multi-marquee spectacular for 35,000 people intended as a showcase for the hardcore dance acts on that label. Unfortunately the event was struck by intimidatingly adverse weather conditions, with constant torrential rain and oppressive tactics by the local establishment who announced on radio that the event had been cancelled. Despite a few of the attractions advertised never materialising, such as The Roman Temple dance arena, there was still a fascinating variety on offer, including fun fair rides, an ambient tent and a Virtual Reality display, all centred around the main stage, which was a mock-Blade Runner affair. The Prodigy were held up outside the venue for two hours by over-zealous security guards and when they finally got on stage it was past 6am. However, the show was well -received, and Keith's antics in the auditorium mud bath proved that, if nothing else, the band were determined to have a good time. The show was an important indication that they were still highly respected within their scene, and that the accusations and recriminations of their detractors concerning their widespread commercial success were not actually given much time by the people closely involved with the underground itself.

This show was paralleled by the band's appearance at Sheffield's Sound City 1992 festival, which was essentially an alternative 'indie' parade. Other bands on the agenda included Ned's Atomic Dustbin, Senseless Things and Suede, so The Prodigy, although not the exception, were certainly not the norm. The audience's warm reception of the gig showed that the band were beginning to span several musical genres with their increasing fan-base, and starting to turn the heads of the cynical and previously unconvinced. The Liverpool show a week later received excellent coverage in the two main music weeklies, who portrayed The Prodigy as something much more substantial than many people gave them credited for, as this review from *NME* shows: "The Prodigy are a riot. Liam Howlett maybe crouched centre stage over his keyboard, but he cleverly compensates by engaging three athletic, flamboyant dancers to embroider his breakbeats. The bare stage suddenly becomes a compulsive multi-faceted entertainment extravaganza. The fascination lies in the layers of sound, the crashing, supremely hedonistic beats which weave to a crazy conclusion. He's a prodigious master of sound. The future is now."

*   *   *

Dance acts don't sell albums. Singles, yes, by the lorry load, but not albums. There is plenty of hard evidence. 1992 had been dance music's most successful year to date, with 17 of the top selling singles of the year making dance the only growth area in a recession-hit and shrinking market. Even so, dance still only accounted for two of the top 40 albums of the same period. Incognito enjoyed a Top 10 hit some months before with their single 'Always There' but their album only peaked at No.44. Similarly, Nomad shifted over 300,000 copies of two top selling singles, but managed only 25,000 sales of their subsequent long player. There is an exception to every rule of course, and bands like Soul II Soul proved that, but generally there was a distinct absence of success for dance albums. When you looked to the more specialist hard dance market, the case was even stronger against artist albums – arguably there were no long players of note whatsoever from this genre.

It was with this established fact in mind that XL only decided to pick up The Prodigy's album option late on. The same was also true for Liam himself, who surprisingly hadn't really considered the possibility until shortly before XL mentioned it: "I hadn't thought of an album until this point, I was quite happy with just a four –single deal. But by now, I had so much new material that releasing just singles would have taken over a year and by then all the stuff would have been out of date. So we decided to put out an album, because it would be a good chance to finally put all this original stuff out there. It was not just a case of banging out twelve tracks however, because at the same time there was the respect and substance that an album requires – to have a successful album can earn serious industry respect, rather than singles success, which is cool but not as important. Having said all this, even when we decided it was time to do an album, the band were still not that fussed about chart positions though, we were all more concerned about knowing the scene and staying true to it."

So with a provisional release date of September 1992, Liam started work on the debut album. Initially he wanted to make a 'rave concept album' along the lines of the early Pink Floyd work, but this idea was shelved once he realised the limitations this might have on his future musical creativity. This approach might tie him too closely to a scene that was dramatically quietening down and, besides, he was no longer inspired by it to the same degree as when he had first started. Considering Liam's highly economical method of working, wherein he can write, record and produce the entire track alone, the actual album's recording was a lengthy process. During the summer of 1992, the band were gigging so frequently that he was rarely given lengthy uninterrupted periods in the studio. Under increasing pressure from the record company to capitalise on the band's high profile and market strength, Liam held out until he felt his work was finished, eventually requiring a total period of six months. The resulting double album, entitled *Experience* (a playful echo of the 1971 Jimi Hendrix posthumous classic) was a brutalist, uncompromising statement, full of hyperspeed breakbeats, bewildering sonic tapestries and thumping rhythms throughout. It offered an 'experience' that both documented the scene the band had emerged from, and offered slight clues as to where they might be heading.

The wailing horns that opened the album with the biblical epic 'Horns Of Jericho' were just a taster of the hour-long blitz of frenetic breakbeats, subliminally deep bass and deliriously fast sonic offerings that were to come. All the singles were there but in re-mixed form, something that Liam's unexploitive nature insisted upon. The version of 'Fire' was far superior to the single mix, whilst a deeply dub version of 'Charly' showed no trace of the cat which by now was well and truly nailed to the studio door. 'Your Love' was refined and classy despite its speed, but perhaps the best re-mix was the near-speed metal treatment of 'Everybody In The Place'. There were several moments of hedonistic ragga, such as 'Ruff In The Jungle Biznezz' and even a live track, 'Death Of The Prodigy Dancers', which offered an insight into the band's live show, although away from the visual spectacular that their PA had now become, this was very weak. In many ways it was a collection of singles, each one a vicious headburst of sound. With few tracks below 145bpm, and with the record being cut over two pieces of vinyl to ensure a loud pressing, this was skillful, mind -bending, high velocity material from start to finish.

That is, except for one track, which in retrospect, was perhaps the most important tune on the album: 'Weather Experience'. The hallucinogenic-style ambience of this track took the listener on a voyage through various climactic experiences, a glorious ultravista that in many ways was an anomaly when placed next to the speeding context of the rest of the album. However, this cinematic, more grandiose track was proof that Liam could write music far outside of the head-down thunderous breakbeat environment that many saw him as typifying. It was his statement that his musical parameters and ambitions were expanding all the time and that he was no longer satisfied with the one dimensionalism of breakbeats. Elsewhere, there was an interesting alchemy of diversity and vision, that is fair to say, but all the forays into musical exploration were essentially tied to the same breakbeat framework, with no tracks other than 'Weather Experience' seriously diverting from the core thrust of the record. In many senses, this was fortunate, for if Liam had indulged in his straining musical flexibility, the record may well have been too diverse and unpalatable for the audience who represented his fan-base at this point. Overall, *Experience* was a very strong debut. Yes, it was limited to a specific breakbeat form, but there was a reassuring complexity at work throughout, and a sense that this was Liam's farewell signal to his birthplace before turning his back and heading off to musical pastures new and far more challenging. The album was the epitome of hardcore at that particular stage, and exactly and absolutely reflected the underground scene from whence The Prodigy came, with just enough variety and experimentalism to avoid being suffocated by that very background. With the caricatures of the band inside the sleeve, there was also a hint that they were already defying those who derided techno as faceless. As such, it was the first real rave album, and therefore seminal by definition, even though it was clearly not just rave. With *Experience* The Prodigy were effectively crowned masters of their genre, and in the process Liam was acknowledged as the most successful writer to emerge for the scene.

The record entered the official album charts at No.12, spent 25 weeks in those listings and sold over 200,000 copies in the UK alone. Aside from the musical achievements of the album, there were certain other important points that were made by *Experience*. Firstly, the record showed that hard dance groups could produce a selection of records on a long player that made a coherent composite, and that maintained their appeal across an hour's worth of music. In many people's eyes, a band is nothing until they have produced a quality album, and The Prodigy had done just that, and in the process consolidated the enormous success and strong fan-base they had established with their impressive string of Top 20 hit singles. It is worth remembering that this record was essentially an instrumental piece, and as such to succeed over this longer form was highly demanding. Thus, it provided a kick in the teeth for those Luddite detractors of hard dance that claimed techno and its musical offshoots were nothing more than a narcotic flash in the pan, a 'soul-less' and transitory musical phase with no longevity. In doing this, the record also answered The Prodigy's own critics who had derided the band because of the existence of musical anomalies like 'Roobarb and Custard'. Also, it was a record that Liam wrote, recorded, engineered and produced himself, another statement of the potential of this form.

The Prodigy

The second major achievement of *Experience* was its seminal nature, and the fact that there were no other comparative albums by the band's musical peer group. Shades of Rhythm and N Joi had not made the impact they had threatened, and rave's court jesters Altern 8 had proved to be of little substance. Nick Halkes of XL remains convinced of the record's unrivalled nature. "I think it was pretty unique in context – other than The Prodigy there wasn't really an artist that came out of that movement that people felt comfortable with, and excited about. *Experience* for me was unique – had N Joi released an album as they could have done six months before, the story might have been different, but they petered out. So there were no real reference points at all. An indication of that is the fact that I was thinking more about how the record stood up to the Kraftwerks of this world. I am not saying The Prodigy reached an incredible pinnacle with *Experience* but it *was* innovative, it was exciting, and it showed there was more depth to the band, and that they could move forward. I wasn't looking too much at the competition simply because there wasn't that much at this stage."

The third and final point of note is that the album succeeded despite the troubles that the scene was experiencing at this stage, which suggests that the band were already appealing to those outside of that scene. The standard of white labels had seriously deteriorated and there was a distinct lack of creativity as well as a musical abuse of the technology available. Commercial forces had almost destroyed the original spirit of the big parties and the ecstasy culture was by now much-maligned, with the majority dismissing the music as no more than a perverse soundtrack to the ecstasy experience, an aural supplement to the chemical changes wrought inside the body by MDMA. Against all these negative factors came The Prodigy album, and it was a considerable achievement. It is important to remember that in discussing these extraneous factors, there is a danger of over-theorising and complicating a musical form that has always been about something more linear and effective – that is, producing good hard dance music. These points are merely suggestions that can place The Prodigy's debut album in a full context and give some indication of the the record's achievements. By the time the next Prodigy album was ready, *Experience* had gone on to sell over 300,000 copies worldwide – so much for dance acts not being able to sell albums.

CHAPTER 5

"Just because everything's not a bed of roses doesn't mean that you are not learning, and that's the best way of looking at things."

Keith

With the successful debut album under their belts, The Prodigy headed out in October for the supporting 23-date British tour, which in many ways was yet another unprecedented step – although the band had played scores of shows since their inception, this was their first actual tour. With them on the road they took their own customised PA, which had been specially imported from the USA for the dates, a 50K Apogee sound system, complete with custom-built interactive modular lighting with 3D heliographic lasers and computer animation, with enough sub-bass to make venues shudder. Also on the tour came support act Sy-Kick, and three DJs,

Devious D, Physics and Ritchie. The Prodigy live show by now was a piercing, vicious live beast, a cauldron of violent sound and high speed visuals that formed an unsettling yet compelling experience. Whilst Liam created the wildly inventive expanses of sound, corralled behind his gear at the back of the stage, Leeroy and Keith engaged in a dancing frenzy, facing each other and mimicking moves crammed with lunatic sleights of foot, just as they used to at The Barn, whilst Maxim roamed the stage overseeing the mayhem. Keith regularly plunged into the crowd, and was often followed by Maxim, leaving Leeroy alone with Liam to keep control. The whole spectacle was daubed in swirling lights and lasers which Liam punched out from his main console. Set against the body-altering frequencies of the ludicrously low sub-bass, the show was a pit of musical psychosis, an unnerving yet compelling sight.

Accompanied everywhere by a haze of sweet smelling smoke and a volley of biting sarcasm and bizarre private jokes, the band worked well under the rigorous conditions of a major tour. Maxim and Liam kept themselves reserved and quiet, as was their nature, whilst Leeroy and Keith took it upon themselves to be the jokers. The first night's show was at Manchester's Hacienda, after which the band played some of the country's biggest venues including Glasgow Barrowlands and Aston Villa Leisure Centre. On the night of the Plymouth show, the band were directed towards their abode for the evening, a tatty bed-and-breakfast on the deserted seafront. There was no-one else working there except a lone Eastern European who was chronically shy and nervous. The band, tired after their energetic show, asked if he had any food available, but he seemed unsure in his reply: "I only started work here tonight, this is my first night of my first job in seven years, which is good, no? I need the money for my wife and seven kids." He then produced the key to the cellar door which Keith hungrily grabbed and promptly disappeared into the depths of the hotel. Twenty minutes later he emerged weighed down with a feast of food, arms filled with loaves, cheese, bacon and ham, vegetables, fruit and dozens of tins, all spilling over his arms. After watching the band scoff the hotel's entire food stocks, the shy waiter wandered over and said, "I think it is best if you pay me a little for all this, or my new boss will be angry. Is £10 too much?"

Leaving Plymouth having probably added one more person to the lengthy dole queue, the band moved on to Scotland, then through East Anglia and the Midlands. At the Coventry show, the band were backstage discussing the night's set list when a stranger walked in and sat alongside them, listening intently. After making an unsuccessful play for Maxim's girlfriend, which did not endear him to the band, the stranger listened for five more minutes and then said, "No, you don't want to do that, drop 'Jericho', replace it with 'Out of Space' and then put 'Everybody In The Place' in at the end." After a pause to admire his handiwork, the unknown advisor then said, "By the way, who are you?" At the show that night, the band's huge sound system proved to be too demanding of the local power supply, so much so that halfway through the set the whole system cut out and

Leeroy backstage.

Maxim, 1992.

Record signing in New York, 1992.

Keith with Moby, 1992.

Leeroy, live at Perception, 1993.

Liam rolling a large roll-up type cigarette
containing a brown, sticky substance.

"Damn you, I'm not afraid of you!"

Liam, Keith and Maxim taking liberties, Australia.

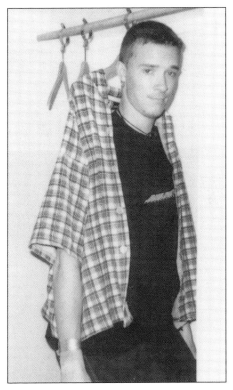

Hanging with Howlett in one of XL's luxury apartments

Liam with his brother in Spain.

Stretching exercises before going on stage.

The Prodigy, early 1994.

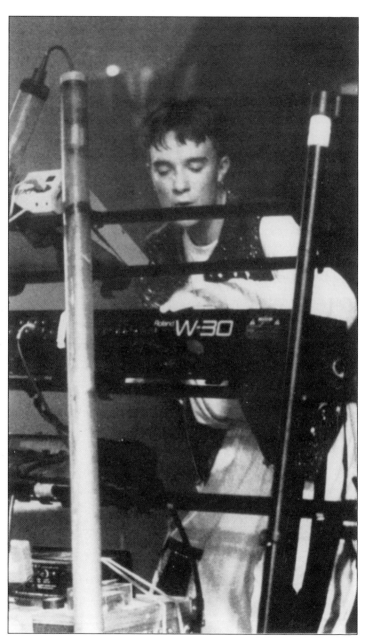

On stage with the trusty Roland W-30

plunged the venue and surrounding city centre into total eerie darkness, after which there was a mini-riot by disappointed fans. On another night, the band were rolling up a joint when the door burst open and four student security guards stormed in, like some ego-bruised rejects from a SWAT team, shouting 'Right, nobody move!' The leader swam his way through the thick haze of smoke from the joints and said, "I think I can smell something strange," smiling all the time in admiration of his incredibly intuitive detective work. He walked around the band taking their joints from them in turn, and placing one in between each finger, so that shortly he was strutting around the changing room, admonishing the band for their habit whilst holding nine joints in his fingers, surrounding himself in a stream of hazy smoke. Such was his indignation that he informed the band he was about to call the police and report them. The Prodigy sat there listening to all this, and when he had finished, Leeroy said, "Okay, call the police then, but you can go and tell the 3000 kids waiting for us to go onstage that the show is off." The embarrassed guard visibly deflated at the prospect and left the room muttering to himself something about "bloody druggies".

The band rolled into Folkestone for the last show of the tour at the Leas Cliff Hall, a venue set into the side of the cliff, such that the roof was actually at foot level for those people walking to the gig along the path above. An hour before the band were due onstage the hall was virtually full and, shortly afterwards, the promoter pinned up the 'Sold Out' notices across all the windows, leaving several hundred disappointed fans outside. The band carried on with their preparations for the show, adjusting the lights and sound mix to get everything perfect. Just as they were finishing their preparations, there was a massive bang from above as a man in a Prodigy T-shirt came crashing through the skylight, sending splinters of glass everywhere; as he whizzed past the balcony he had tried to land on, he smashed headfirst onto the mixing desk, where he lay unconscious and twitching. The band and a stunned engineer ran over to the man, who by now had fallen on to the floor in a bloody heap, and was beginning to regain consciousness. His face was badly cut and already swelling with the sizeable bruises from his fall, and his trousers were soaking from the contents of his emptied bladder which he had been unable to control on the way down. When the man turned to face the band he had been so desperate to see, his face was covered with dents of mixing desk knobs from where he had crunched into them. The damage to the mixing desk itself was even more severe and the band had to play the entire show through just eight of the original 32 channels. As if he had not been through enough already, the fall guy was hurriedly dragged to the changing rooms by the venue security, whereupon the police arrived and arrested him for criminal damage, took him to the station and kept him there all night, still in his piss-stained trousers and mixing desk-shaped face. He missed the entire show.

This ill-fated display of fascination in The Prodigy was a factor with which the band were not always comfortable. Obviously they were pleased that people could be into the band so much, but there was an uneasiness about the celebrity that was inevitably associated with this degree of loyalty. Their anti-star attitude had already been amply displayed in many ways: their continued refusal to play *Top of the Pops*, their encouragement of mainstream radio not to play their tracks, and their continued habit of dancing in the crowd as soon as they had left the stage were just a few indications of their complete and unreserved rejection of any celebrity. This distaste for the fame game was an inherent feature of The Prodigy, and one that was not about to disappear because of their success. On the contrary, as their profile increased and album sales grew, the band became more and more repulsed by the whole idea of celebrity, and on this tour they were unhappy when it did rear its ugly head, as Leeroy explains: "Sometimes it's annoying that you can't go out there and just have a dance, because you will get treated differently. That spoils it for us, we don't want to be stars, we want none of all that. We have time for everyone. You have to acknowledge the people who see you as stars as well, but that doesn't make us comfortable with it, not at all. I would much rather people met us and came away surprised by our lack of celebrity. There is no room for stars in our scene and there never has been. There is no star-making machinery other than a few flyers with DJs names on there, but even then you don't see people like Carl Cox as a star, but just as a DJ who makes you buzz. People want to dance and get a buzz, not have some inflated star ego parade in front of them. That is the way our scene sees it, that is the way we have always seen it, and I can't ever see that changing."

In many senses, the 'Experience' tour was a great

success for The Prodigy, with good crowd reactions which healthily fuelled the album sales. However, it was not all a rosy picture. Many shows were far from sold-out – the opening night at Manchester's Hacienda, for example, was only half full with just over 500 people, and other nights were worse. The band were repeatedly disheartened to meet people in the street on the night of a show and find that these youngsters didn't even know The Prodigy were in town. With many local rave promoters being relatively inexperienced in this area of tour organisation, there was a serious lack of marketing and promotion for some shows. This was exacerbated by the general incompatibility between the way the shows were organised and the culture and musical background the band's fan-base expected – to a certain degree these were still put on as rave nights, but the shows were frequently too early and too expensive. Maybe the idea of a hard dance band on tour was still too new to be readily accepted. Whatever the reasons for these failures, the financial consequences for the band were dire – they returned home after a hard month on the road deeply in debt. Furthermore, this was new territory to The Prodigy, who had previously only known the buzz of ascendancy and a long running series of successes – this was perhaps their first major step backwards. Still, the band reconciled themselves with the fact that the tour *had* helped sell many more albums, and there had been some very encouraging crowds. After all, in the popular music press there were fashionable bands playing to 150 screaming girls at tiny secret locations and being credited with a youth explosion, yet here were The Prodigy, relatively undocumented, pulling crowds of 1000 on their bad nights. So perhaps it was not all bad news. And besides, the band had an Australasian and American tour to look forward to after Christmas.

★   ★   ★

The band flew out to Melbourne on Boxing Day 1992. On tour in Australia they joined Sasha and Paul Oakenfold, which proved to be an unusual and perhaps ill-advised mix of styles. After a few mixed reactions, Keith became concerned that the choice of line-up had indeed been ill-conceived. He worried that fans of The Prodigy would find Oakenfold's music too mellow, and conversely, that Oakenfold's fans would be turned off by the harder sound of The Prodigy. After another tepidly received show, Keith was talking to Mike about exactly this problem, with particular reference to Oakenfold's suspected playing of Sesame Treet's 'Trip To Trumpton' on New Year's Eve. As Keith finished off the conversation, he started to back out of Mike's room into the corridor, but was too busy talking to notice the DJ he was criticising, Paul Oakenfold, standing there about to enter his room. At that exact moment, Keith waved goodbye to his manager and shouted, "Right, I'm off to see DJ Floor Clearer."

Leeroy did not enjoy these dates and the subdued reactions to their show: "They weren't ready for it, they didn't really understand where we were coming from. They were into techno, and that was that. I didn't really enjoy it as a result." Tired, but with the five Australian

The Prodigy

dates completed, the band flew straight to America to begin a heady 28 date tour in 30 days, with the two days off being used to record the video for their next single 'Wind It Up'. This next month was to be one of the band's strangest and most difficult since they had started. In many ways it provided some of the highlights of their career so far. In other ways, it nearly threatened their very existence.

The tour was not short of eventful incidents. Unfortunately, after only a few hours driving, the tour bus spluttered to a halt and stubbornly refused to restart. With several hundred miles still to go, the band were staring at a possible cancellation, but after hasty calculations were made, it became clear that the financial repercussions of not playing the show would cost them more than hiring a commuter plane to get there in time. To a band entrenched in self-sufficiency, this all whiffed of rock-star antics, but they bowed to necessity and headed for the small local airport. By the time they arrived, they had all conjured up visions of an executive hi-tech jet with televisions and individual hostess service. They asked which plane they had booked and the tour manager pointed to a small dishevelled hangar, out of which was being pushed a battered old propeller plane, complete with scrappy paint-work and bald tyres, about the size of their tour bus. The plane was so small that Keith had to get in first and sit in the very crevice of the tail, so that there was enough room for Leeroy, who spent the entire flight doubled up at the front. The violent turbulence soon silenced any false bravado amongst the band, and soon after Keith could be heard pleading from the back for the pilot to "fly lower, this is like a flying bath." Finally landing with a bump and a communal sigh of relief, the band headed for the near-jeopardized show and were welcomed by a British ex-pat who offered them what he called "tastes of home", and promptly handed them a sack of magic mushrooms, a bag of weed and some Marmite.

Despite the hectic travel problems, the show went well, after which the band retired to the repaired tour bus and prepared themselves for yet another lengthy drive. The bus itself was owned by The Eagles and was emblazoned with its name along the bodywork – 'Hotel California'. After the stresses of the last few days The Prodigy set about enjoying their tastes of home and within minutes they had taken all the mushrooms whilst the weed was rolled up and smoked in abundance. With The Prodigy on tour was Moby, the health conscious, vegetarian, non-smoking, non-drugging musician, whose quarters were at the front end of Hotel California, with The Prodigy's considerably more depraved dwelling at the back. Over the next month a suffering Moby spent most of his time asking them to shut their door, whilst stuffing his door edges with blankets and paper to stop the myriad of illegal fumes emanating from the den of inequity at the back.

In Los Angeles, there were several noted luminaries in the crowd including Rick Rubin of Def Jam fame, Ian Astbury of The Cult, Grace Jones and Bill Gibbons from ZZ Top. However, it was the unwanted attentions of a complete stranger which became the evening's most memorable moment. The band were sitting backstage, collecting their thoughts after the show, when Liam noticed a strange man watching them through a mirror which reflected who was in the changing room through a crack in the door. When the man continued looking at them oddly for over twenty minutes the band began to wonder what he was up to, so they invited him in. Liam went over, shook his hand and said, "Hi, I'm Liam" and the man (whom by now they had realised was obviously tripping on acid) just stopped dead in his tracks, gaped his mouth wide open in astonishment and put his head in his hands, before turning and walking out without saying a word. The band followed him out whereupon he turned to Liam, smiled and said, "Steve, you're my brother man, Steve, it's me." Since Liam had no brothers, was not in the habit of calling himself Steve and had never seen this man before, the band spent the next thirty minutes trying to convince the man of his mistake, but each time he would say, "Steve, how are you, my man? You're my brother man." By now the band were a little spooked out, so Liam decided to placate his supposed sibling and agree that he was in fact his brother. This did not deter the stranger, who ignored Liam's concession and continued with his rantings, interspersed every few sentences with "Steve, man". Eventually, Liam's erstwhile brother had to be forcibly ejected from the venue, an act of family betrayal that did not go unnoticed, as the oddball walked off down the road mumbling, "How could you do this to me Steve? You're my brother man."

In Dallas, the band were checking in at the reception of their hotel, when they noticed the apparent absence of any other guests, but put this down to their late arrival and the fact it was a mid-week. They quickly unpacked and headed into town for a relaxing drink. As they walked up the road away from the hotel, Keith looked back and noticed that, but for their own rooms, the hotel was in complete darkness – theirs were the only bookings in a 350-room building. During their entire stay they never saw another guest. After an uneasy night's drinking, they returned and were shown around the executive suite by the elderly lady who ran the ghost hotel. The suite was unchanged since the 1970s, including thick shag carpets and art decor, and appeared not to have been used for many years. A nervous night's sleep was followed by an even more unsettling start to the day. Maxim went to breakfast with Keith and was about to order his meal when the old lady appeared from nowhere and said, "You'll want eggs and bacon, one slice of toast and a coffee with one sugar." Her selection was absolutely right, but before that could sink in she turned to Keith and said, "And you'll be wanting two eggs, sausages with tomatoes, and tea, white with no sugar." Again correct. She then took the menus from the stunned friends, and retired to the empty kitchen to prepare their food.

A later show was at The Lizard Lounge, which had formerly been the site of legendary gigs by The Doors. This gig proved to be the highlight of this American tour and one of the best shows The Prodigy had ever played up until then – the band were so impressed by the enthusiasm of the crowd that they played the set through twice. Ten minutes before they were due on stage, Leeroy had stood up to stretch, and in the process had snapped his trouser elastic, whereupon they fell round his ankles.

The Prodigy

He had hurriedly wound some gaffer tape across his midriff to secure his trousers in time for the show. Once onstage however, every time he leant down the trousers stuck higher and higher up his frame, until at the end of the show they were crammed right up the cheeks of his bottom and he looked like a seven-foot schoolboy in knee-length shorts. Still, he was not alone in his comical outfit – at the same show Maxim had forgotten to remove the dry cleaning label from his red costume, and so spent the entire night MC-ing to this ultimate hardcore dance music with a piece of paper stuck to his back saying '40 degrees, Drip Dry, Collect Tuesday'.

Leeroy's clothing troubles were not over just yet. At another show, he had lost his luggage, so the only clothes available were those he was standing in, a pair of jeans and a T-shirt. With no other option but to wear them, he pulled out his trusty gaffer tape again, and stuck a strip down the outside of each leg. Halfway through the show the tape became unstuck in the middle but not at the top and bottom, so when Leeroy spun around he looked like a deformed MC Hammer with big baggy jodhpurs. His embarrassment quickly turned to hysterics after the show, when a shy girl approached him and asked him where he had bought the trendy pantaloons.

Before another show, the band were sitting in the hotel's reception when a stranger walked over and introduced himself as Jeff, and sat next to Maxim. On tour dozens of people introduced themselves all the time so the band thought nothing of this, and besides, he seemed nice enough. He also seemed to get on particularly well with Maxim: "He stayed and talked to me and the band for quite a while, and we were cool with that, he seemed okay. Then I needed the toilet but when I mentioned this and stood up to go, he stood up as well and said, 'Do you want me to come with you?' It was only then that I realised he was moving in on us! We made our excuses and retired to our rooms." Maxim's room was adjoining Liam's and was separated only by a partition door, so the MC waited for Liam to settle down and then rang his hotel room phone. Liam answered the call and Maxim, disguising his voice, said, "Hi, it's Jeff, can I come up to your room? I know I was talking to your friend, but I really like you, man." Before a startled Liam had chance to answer, the voice on the other end of the phone said, "I'm on my way up, see you in a second." Liam suspected Maxim immediately, so he went through into the next room, but Maxim appeared to be fast asleep on the couch, so Liam nervously returned to his own bedroom. In the meantime, Maxim had waited for Liam to leave and then rushed out into the corridor, knocked on his door and seductively said "Hi, Liam, it's Jeff, I'm here, let me in." Liam spent the night firmly barricaded in his room waiting for the dreaded knock on his door to go away. The night of the actual show, the band's huge, tattooed and muscular merchandise man was the subject of a somewhat less friendly proposition. A nasty-looking character had been watching the healthy T-shirt sales all night and when there were only a few people around he walked over and said, "What if I was to jump over this table and steal all your money?" The merch-man stood up to his full impressive height, pulled out a handgun and said,

"I'd blow your brains out." The guy, a little unnerved but nevertheless obviously desperate, replied, "Well, you might miss ..." The reply came back, "Not fifteen times."

The day after the show, the band checked out of their hotel and headed into town for a quick snack before their next journey. The pretty blonde waitress took their orders and, noticing their accents, she said in a thick Southern drawl, "Yous all ain't from round here, is yee?" They told her they were a band and tried in vain to explain what sort of music The Prodigy played, but decided that now was not the time to enter into a lengthy debate about the relative merits of Belgian industrial techno over German house. It was probably just as well – her bemused face gave away the fact that she clearly had absolutely no comprehension of what they were talking about. She patiently waited until they had finished and then simply said, "I ain't heard of none of that, boys. I only listen to two types of music. Country and Christian."

In some ways, this hilarious incident was indicative of a real problem the band had in America – there was only a limited awareness of their music and they had to work hard to convince people of their worth. Although Belgium's LA Style had already become the first techno -derivative band to break the *Billboard* Top 100 singles chart with 'James Brown Is Dead', the genre was still relatively unknown. In addition, the American consumer media had already noticed the possibility for scandal that these so-called 'raves' offered, and they fed off the drug stories and illegal parties as hungrily as their British counter-parts. Undercover police would regularly attend the parties, and the authorities monitored the scene as closely and with the same zest with which they scrutinised hip-hop lyrics. This general air of misinformation and uncertainty about the scene made some nights quite awkward for the band. Even so, there were still hotbeds of interest and although it was a smaller, more college-oriented following, the band were met with excellent reactions in places such as LA, Maine, New York, Texas and Detroit.

Despite all these comical incidents and exciting times for the band, there was unfortunately a very serious underlying concern – the financial returns that the band had hoped for failed to materialise. However, the band were effectively forced into submission by the possible legal repercussions of cancelling shows at such a late stage. As a result, the band immediately found themselves living off their own money instead and their reluctance to let their fans down meant they felt they had to continue nevertheless. After only one show Leeroy announced he was going home unless things were sorted out – promises were hastily made and he was placated, but circumstances never improved. Five of these shows were effectively played for free.

This disheartening development was paralleled by the band's deteriorating health. Since The Prodigy had started, their career had been a whirlwind of PAs and video shoots, but now, finally, the exertions began to take their inevitable toll. There had only been six days off in the last 100 days, and now they had to shoot the 'Wind It Up' video on two of those. They had started the rigorous American leg of the tour tired and ill, having flown from Australia with a show the same night, and it never really improved from there. Consequently, they all developed serious bouts of 'flu and other debilitating ailments. In Toronto, Maxim was so ill with bronchitis that he had to miss the show, and Leeroy was forced to improvise and become MC for the night, despite being under the weather himself. Liam and Keith were similarly run down, with all four of the band regularly leaving the stage between songs to vomit or lie down. The band were finishing gigs coughing and seeing stars, whilst people were shoving paperwork under their running noses and bleary eyes saying, "You've got to play this show." The threats worked, as Keith explains: "It sounds really false but we were thinking, 'We can't let the people down, we have to play these shows,' so that was that. We played them, inspite of everything." The situation was becoming intolerable. They couldn't understand what was happening, this was not how The Prodigy worked, they were used to buzzing off each other and loving every minute of the band. Now they felt frustrated, angry, ill and helpless. They had done their side of the deal and performed well every night, despite their ill health and financial woes. At times during this American tour, all four members swore they were leaving the band and flying home. By the time the dates were completed, they were mentally and physically ravaged, deep in debt and morale was at an all-time low.

★   ★   ★

On their return, the band took a few weeks off to recuperate. They had no money in their pockets to show for their troubles and the debts from the UK tour were still around. It was a deeply depressing period. Over time, the band gradually began to face up to what had happened and rationalise their experience and eventually they managed to put the US tour into perspective and learn from what had happened. Keith speaks for the rest of the band when he looks back on that difficult period: "We should have known really because of the way Leeroy reacted – he's so laid-back, and you know that if he is unhappy and miserable with something, then there is a very real problem. We said we were never going to tour again after that, we were *so* pissed off, 70 gigs over Christmas and the New Year and yet we still come home in debt. We were all very run down, which was no wonder because our schedules had been so hectic for so long. Of course, that compounded the situation because it is always difficult to deal with things mentally if you are feeling so low physically. Over time, we felt better and began to prioritise events – it proved to us that we are so strong as a band that ultimately money doesn't come into it. We had come through that nasty situation and we were stronger as a band for the experience. We made a lot of big buzzes out of a lot of skinny situations on that tour, it pulled us together, and we should be proud as a band because of that. I enjoyed being with all those people but the tour was hard. People say touring must be a great laugh and the easy life. Well, you imagine saying to someone, 'Right, me and you are going out 28 times in the next 30 days and every night we are going to come home so tired we'll barely be able to walk.' Now not everybody sees it like that, it can be very rigorous.

The Prodigy

"A few weeks after we returned home we were all awarded a gold disc for sales of the album, which cheered us up no end, but some of the executives used that as a battering ram to justify all that we had been through. They'd say, 'Yes, it's difficult, but touring achieves all these sales,' that sort of routine. They weren't the ones out there and no-one patted us on the back for our work and admitted that they had made mistakes. We were getting £30 a night and then being told what to think by these outsiders and that was really poor. Yes, the album sold well, but *Liam* did that, Liam wrote it, Liam put the concept together, *Liam fucking did it*, with help from us three. Liam did it with the help of three really loyal friends. I enjoyed the tour, it was hard work with such a lot of dates, but it definitely did no end of good for the band. Unfortunately it wasn't quite right somewhere along the line. Now we look back at the whole episode in retrospect as a trial and as a learning experience. Just because everything's not a bed of roses doesn't mean that you are not learning, and that's the best way of looking at things like that."

CHAPTER 6

"The old style was wearing very thin by now and I realised that the band had to progress and evolve, that I had to get back to the music and move forward. I felt 'One Love' was perhaps the first time that we had really pioneered and moved on substantially from where we had originated. It was a big jump."

Liam

Liam had just turned off the M11 and begun driving towards home along the deserted A-road, when in front of his car he saw an ostrich, head swaying up and down as the gargantuan bird jumped along the tarmac. He blinked and looked again, and it was still there. He and his mates were on their way back from a big outdoor party and it was nearly 6am in the morning, so Liam was obviously a little surprised to be confronted by an eight-foot bird apparently heading for the motorway junction. His mates had all been heavily indulging in acid, and as Liam looked in the rear view mirror, one particularly badly drugged friend woke up, looked out of the car window and saw an African ostrich stop by the vehicle and lower its head to look in. This was too much, and the shaken man started gibbering about having taken drugs one time too many, and that his hallucinations were getting more and more realistic with each trip. After a few seconds surveying the occupants of the car, the ostrich headed off towards the motorway, probably to get a sandwich from the nearby service station. Liam, still stunned, headed home and the next morning told his dad about his weird night out. His father, used to Liam coming home from all-night raves in various states, listened to his son's story of the big bird and simply nodded, "Yeah, sure Liam," then carried on eating his breakfast.

What had actually happened was that the ostrich had escaped from a local bird sanctuary and was eventually caught by dozens of police, heading for Cambridge in the fast lane of the M11. What it provided Liam with was an unusual addition to the video for the single 'Out Of Space', which was released whilst the band had been on tour in support of the *Experience* album, in November 1992. As well as the ostriches, the usual feast of dancing and the footage of Prodigy live shows, the video also featured shots of Keith dressed up as the archetypal raver, complete with face mask, white overalls, Vicks Vapor Rub and florescent gloves. For some reason, Altern 8 took this as an offensive slur on their own band's costumery and for their next video they dressed themselves up as The Prodigy. The band's single became their fifth consecutive Top 15 hit, not bad for an act whose success had originally been deemed as too instant to last – The Prodigy were never supposed to stay around this long. The track 'Out Of Space' was one of the strongest on the album, and with its heavy ragga influence gave the release an individuality that worked well. The hardcore junglism was abruptly punctuated by the core sample, which was a Max Romeo phrase from 'Chase The Devil', and its refrained use showed Liam's intention not to abuse sampling technology, but to use the sections creatively and with respect to the original artist. The element of dissonance that is in so many Prodigy tracks was also there, again lending it that eerie, unearthly feel that had almost become Liam's trademark. On the flip side was a tougher 'Techno Underworld Mix' and a live version of 'Music Reach 1234', which again offered an insight into the band's powerful live performance. It was an inventive record and thus kept the band's considerable momentum moving forward.

Their next single release was in March 1993, after returning from the strenuous American tour, but 'Wind It Up' did nothing to further The Prodigy's creative development, despite selling well once again. Although the track itself was reasonable enough, this was their most throwaway single, because it was the sound of the band treading water. Worse still, the detrimental effect of releasing another breakbeat track was something that they had all been more than aware of, but circumstances prevented them from avoiding this trap. After 'Out Of

Space', the band had come to realise the inherent danger in using breakbeats for too much longer, and Liam had even appeared in the press hinting that The Prodigy's music was under-going a very drastic transformation. During the autumn of 1992, the big rave boom had seriously started to dwindle, and by the time 'Wind It Up' was released there was growing concern for the wilting appeal and limited shelf-life of the scene. With the increased government and police activity against the big parties exacerbating the growing discredit of the form, the 'rave' banner was in grave danger of becoming a crippling albatross for The Prodigy, and threatened to drag them down with its own rotting corpse. Breakbeats were a quintessential part of this. The Prodigy knew the scene was becoming a self-parody, a joke, and that there was a real danger of artistic suffocation if they remained too closely linked to that. Also, with the extensive travelling they had done in recent months, they had been exposed to a brave new world of music, which inevitably influenced the way they were thinking and ideas for new material. However, 'Wind It Up' was still released, and continued down the path of breakbeats. What were The Prodigy doing?

The problem with the travelling and rigorous schedules of the last year was that although they broadened their musical horizons enormously, they also limited the amount of time that Liam was able to work in the studio, and hence restricted his opportunities to create new work. In so doing, the more they travelled and gigged, the less chance he had of moving The Prodigy onwards and evolving in the fashion they wanted.

Consequently, just before the end of 1992 when the record company asked him for the next single, in order to keep the band's profile high, he had nothing new to offer. They wanted 'Wind It Up' but he was very unhappy with the choice, it was too breakbeat, too 'rave', even too dated – a step backwards in effect, and possibly a very perilous one. Unfortunately, Liam could not come up with any viable alternative, as schedules continued to deny him access to studio time, so in the end, and with great reluctance he agreed to release 'Wind It Up'.

The video for the track, as mentioned earlier, was shot during the band's lengthy American tour on two of their three days off, in various locations in and around Los Angeles, including Venice Beach and Death Valley. The video company drove around the city stopping off when they saw appropriate locations, such as a Christmas tree which Keith duly attacked with relish. Another such spot was a bank of enormous boulders that acted as a wave break on Venice Beach. Keith was the least tired of the four and seemed to have loads of ideas for this video, so he suggested that he stand on the rocks and be filmed as these huge waves broke over his back. He instructed the band and crew to tell him when the waves were coming so he could brace himself for the considerable impact. The first three waves went okay, Keith watched for the warning from the band and the footage was captured. Then Keith noticed that the other three seemed to be standing still and silent, and wondered why – he had no time to think however, as the immense 20-foot wave that smashed into him (and had scared his friends into silence) swept him off the rocks. He gripped on for dear life and swallowed lung-fulls of salt water, then dropped to the ground and stumbled his way to the beach, still stunned and with his arms covered in grazes and bruises, before collapsing in front of the cameraman. Keith lay there, dazed and hyperventilating, but the director looked at him, said, "Cut, that was great!" and walked off.

It was a good video but Liam was still not happy. It was not that the track was substandard, far from it. With the piano breakbeats and ragga vocals it confirmed their status a the UK's top hard dance act by smashing into the charts at No.11. With the hard and fast 'We Are The Ruffest' on the flip-side and maniac ambient and percussive remixes as well, it was a consistent and solid record. However, this was the fifth single from the album, something that Michael Jackson was at the time being heavily chastised for with his album *Dangerous*. Liam knew he could have done better given the time, and the fear that he was beginning to carry a breakbeat millstone around his neck plagued him constantly. Although it was only one release, Liam now recognises that 'Wind It Up' could have scuppered their growing reputation as an innovative and progressive act: "I could have written something better than that as a single. Around that time we were looking to change the music, to get away from the breakbeat and do something a bit more techno. We were listening to all this music from abroad which we had heard whilst touring, as well as guitar bands like Nirvana, all sorts of stuff. 'Wind It Up' was written over a year before its release when I was also writing tracks like 'Fire', and so it simply did not reflect the dozens of new influences that I was listening to. I was really unhappy about that. I regret that release even though it did well in the charts, because it did absolutely nothing for our long-term development, and possibly even threatened that. It was a gamble that just about came off, but I was pissed off with it, and I could have written much better. At that point, there was an air of claustrophobia developing around the band, in that I felt the records and videos were sounding and looking the same. We knew that we had to get away from the whole rave thing, because it was in grave danger of killing the band's future creativity." Keith succinctly sums up their growing concern about the band's visual presentation at this same stage: "You imagine the night down the pub when you got pissed and did the John Travolta splits, an hour of pub singing and generally acting really badly, then you wake up the next day and think 'Oh shit, everybody saw that'. Well, if you do a video for MTV then everybody *will* see it, and what's more, hundreds of times! It is really hard at first to get used to that idea, and inevitably that has to make you more careful about how you present the band to people." At the same time, they were not compromising their central dislike of the star-making machinery of the industry, as Liam explains: "Ever since the band started, there has been a very strong desire to avoid any celebrity and any element of being 'stars'. That is not us, that is totally at odds with how we think. The anti-star element is always there, but it took 'Wind It Up' to make us realise that our credibility was in danger of falling off. We had credibility in the scene and we weren't looking to get *any* respect outside of that scene. And as far as being stars goes – no thanks."

The Prodigy

*   *   *

During the summer of 1993 there was a promotional white label hard house tune circulating around the underground scene by a band calling themselves Earthbound, with two versions available. The record arrived cheaply packaged and with someone's home address hastily scribbled on the label. Despite the spartan packaging, reactions to these records were very enthusiastic, with all the major DJs of note picking up on them, and crowd reactions were similarly positive. One dance magazine even went as far as to say, "This is the best white label we have received this year." The track's Arabic muezzin-punctuated hardcore, with its percussion laden and bouncy bassline was an impressive mixture. Earthbound 2 was mellower, more tranced and chilled, but equally effective. The unearthly voices across the record were complemented by classical sweeps and hard pulsing house beats, but all controlled with an admirable degree of finesse. Clearly, Earthbound was a new act with enormous potential. There was much discussion about who Earthbound were, yet no-one knew or guessed. When the writer of these tracks was finally made known to the public, there was much consternation by the underground scene snobs who had derided The Prodigy for many months because of their commercial success. The record they were now hailing as the year's best white label was in fact a product of Liam Howlett's very own Earthbound studios, and the tracks were from the forthcoming release by The Prodigy.

The pseudonym and white label ploy was deliberate, simple and utterly effective. Such was the disdain which certain luminaries of the underground viewed The Prodigy's widespread commercial success, that by the release of 'Out Of Space' there was little chance that any of the band's records would be given a fair hearing and certainly even less chance that they would be spun on those preciously pretentious turntables, where suitability was often judged more on the scarcity of a dub plate than on a track's actual worth. Once the music press had filled its pages with excellent reviews of the Earthbound release, there was now clear evidence that The Prodigy were in fact capable of producing innovative and pioneering dance music, and that this fact would have to be recognised once the scene snobs had seen past their frail and limited vision. The shock to these people was considerable, but unfortunately their myopic musical attitudes were then confirmed when they immediately stopped playing Earthbound 1 and 2 once it had been confirmed it was actually Liam. Their shock was probably matched by that of The Prodigy's hardcore following – this was a radical and complete departure from anything the band had released thus far (the white labels now command prices in the region of £120 each in the collector's market). The band had wanted the previous release to be a step forward, but that had never materialised; now the new record, retitled 'One Love' was just such a directional break, as Liam explains: "'One Love' was quite a big jump. It was more of a housey tune, less breakbeats, and that could have lost us all the people who had previously followed us for the breakbeat element. In a way, the whole scene at that point was confused, unsure, and as such was splitting up into various categories, with one set of DJs going one way and others going elsewhere. I didn't want to get involved in all the internal politics, because that would have restricted me creatively, I would have been too limited. So 'One Love' came from that. With the more typical Prodigy 'Full Throttle' and the B-side incorporating the Johnny L mixes, which were more German techno with a touch of breakbeat, it was still a hard record. That whole EP was a strong sign that we wanted to do things differently. The old style was wearing very thin by now and we were very lucky to get away with 'Wind It Up'. After my uneasiness with that previous single, I realised that the band had to progress and evolve, that I had to get back to the music and move forward."

Clues to this sharp change could have been gleaned from the re-mixes Liam chose to do during the summer of 1993, which although were harder than 'One Love', they offered signs that Liam was flexing his creative muscles in many directions. The first remix, for pop techno band Jesus Jones (who played the *Experience* album non-stop on their American tour bus) was an unusually commercial choice perhaps, but Liam produced such a bombastic, brutal and even violent re-mix that many people had to reconsider their earlier reservations. It was the second remix though, of Belgian meister-stompers Front 242's 'Religion' that won Liam genuine and widespread acclaim, a remix full of immense, yet sophisticated terror. *Mixmag* was now forced to admit the quality of Liam's work on the Front

242 remix: "Incredible. Absolutely incredible. Terror hard stomping first mix, immense. Liam Howlett is a genius. This is it." The industry rumours that he was venturing deep into the hard and bleak world of techno were fuelled even more by these two impressive remixes.

The reasons for this change in direction and the resultant broadening of The Prodigy's musical palate were manifold. Firstly, as briefly mentioned before, the band's extensive touring had exposed them to all manner of new music that they might otherwise not have heard had they stayed in Essex or England. The thriving European dance scene had German techno, Belgium industrial and a whole host of other interesting material. America, Australia and even Japan all offered something new, and not just dance music, but also Sub Pop-style guitar bands, ambient, and funk to name but a few. For Liam his desire to expand and develop was increasing at an alarming rate, and this transitional phase was a crucial time: "I just felt there was so much music to listen to and learn from. I wanted to stop using speeded up hip-hop samples and start writing music in a slightly different way. It's all to do with travelling around and getting inspiration from all sorts of music. There were no particular bands I would highlight, we just realised that from touring that there was so much more music out there. The breakbeat is such an English scene, and London is the centre of that, and there is so much more out there to listen to and to write. With 'One Love', I felt this was perhaps the first time that we had really pioneered and moved on substantially from where we had originated. It was a big jump."

Maxim agrees that they were all into much more varied music now and remembers what he thought when he first heard the new track: "Those tracks on that EP just blew my mind, it was like nothing I had ever heard before, just the hardest tunes, especially 'Rhythm of Life'. Then he came out with 'One Love', another style again. He has his own style, but not like one that I have ever heard before, it all sounds like Liam, the way he does things is totally original. People say there shouldn't be categories in music, and they always ask us which one do we fit in – well, Liam has such a maverick, individual quality that for me he has effectively created his own category."

This was an important element of the second reason why The Prodigy changed direction at this point – the *Experience* album was now left far behind, which was just as well, because the scene it had originated from was finally petering out during 1993. The old sound and spirit could not have been recaptured if The Prodigy had wanted to, and the myriad of changes on the scene, musically and elsewhere complicated what was already a messy death. Major festivals and parties were continually being arranged and then cancelled at the very last minute, law suits flew across the country from one angry promoter to another and back. Cocaine had now become readily available as a deviant on the original drug culture. As a result, the Summer of Love had become the summer of failure. The Prodigy's evolution away from this scene coincided with its ultimate demise.

Thirdly, the band realised that visually it was time that they moved on and changed. Their videos, although entertaining, had thus far been essentially all of the same vein, dance promos with little or no story or band involvement other than their actual dance moves. So for this record, the band dropped all the costumes ("we were into it at the time, but we no longer fancied looking like The Stylistics") and had their long locks chopped. Stage-wear began to resemble a hard street look rather than any premeditated image. Press exposure was cut back severely, to avoid over-exposure. Perhaps the most crucial visual development was the video for 'One Love' itself, which was a radical change from anything they had done before. Using a brand new computer package from the United States, the band created a splendid Aztec-style city, a visual feast of hi-tech graphics and computer reality to accompany the breakthrough track. Their appearances in the video were limited to only a few computer-simulated dance moves, and Keith was featured for no more than three seconds at the very end of the piece. The new directors seemed to understand the band's desire to move on and progress and they worked well together. As a result, MTV picked up on the video and gave it heavy rotation, something that had eluded the band so far, and this subsequently exposed their music to a whole new fan-base of people. This, tied in with 'One Love's more 4/4 European slant, meant that the band suddenly found themselves with a growing following on the Continent. All these reasons give an insight into The Prodigy's notable shift in their musical vision at the time of 'One Love', although the evolution was more gradual and natural than this rather clinical breakdown suggests. The core point is that by now, The Prodigy were a band that had proved themselves capable of musical and visual growth, and in turn had opened the eyes of their fan-base and a whole new following to the enormous creative potential of the act. The shift in emphasis worked – when 'One Love' was released in October 1993, the record reached No.8 in the charts, but more importantly earned The Prodigy a great deal more respect than any of their previous records. The tide of opinion both underground and otherwise was finally turning in the band's favour.

★　★　★

The summer and autumn of 1993 was spent playing yet more PAs, which coincided with the lengthy absence of recorded material prior to the release of 'One Love'. In that period, the band played over sixty shows, and complemented their growing international appeal with more shows abroad, especially in Europe. They played the massive Mayday festival in Germany, a show in Athens and dates in Ireland, Japan, Holland, Belgium, and Denmark. In Britain, one of these earlier shows was at the massive Resurrection outdoor party in Edinburgh, and it was here that The Prodigy felt the full force of the new sweeping, anti-party laws that were being introduced, and would soon take shape under the banner of The Criminal Justice Bill. With the band headlining the huge show watched by 12,000 people, there was a sound level monitor man with headphones stalking the festival site with a decibel reader; whenever he felt the volume exceeded the legal limit he insisted that the band's sound system was turned down. Since the legal limit was a paltry 95 Db (which meant that if a plane flew overhead it would completely drown out the band), this was a serious restriction on The Prodigy's performance, made all the more annoying because there were no residential buildings within five miles of the site. After half an hour of trying to perform under these limiting conditions, The Prodigy did something they had never done before – they walked off stage and stopped the show. There was great unrest and discontentment in the crowd, matched by the anger of the band themselves, who were incensed by the severity of the regulations, exacerbated by the show's potential to have been one of their best ever. By this stage, crippling fines, equipment seizures and licence revocations were commonplace, so the event promoters had no choice but to co-operate with the monitor man and turn the band down. Already the authorities had forced the culture overground by demanding licences and legalised raves, which were always going to be a poor imitation of the original spirit; now they were enforcing even harsher regulations on the events that were authorised as well. It was a no-win situation.

As a result of this disappointing debacle, The Prodigy issued a one page statement to the press, which mirrored one that was then released on the 'One Love' record sleeve. In it, the band laid the blame for the current problems of the scene squarely at the feet of the Department of Health and Environment whose regulations and Db meters caused all the trouble, and went on to apologise to the fans for the poor sound quality and short set. The record statement went on to

The Prodigy

clarify The Prodigy's beliefs and intentions in the form of a message to its followers and everyone involved in dance: "Forget the authorities, you can't stop us, we're gonna keep the dance scene strong even if the world isn't. This is your day and no-one can take it away from you. The dance scene is too strong to disappear."

The Marquee, February 1994.

"Honestly, Officer, I haven't taken a thing ..."

Keith, cone-head, Australia, 1994.

Donald Gorgon.

Keith checking out the buzz of the crowd, 1994.

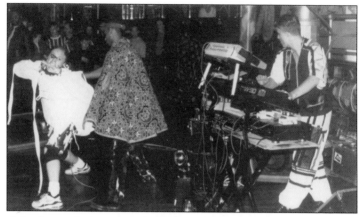

Maxim assisting a strait-jacketed Keith on stage, 1994 ...

... while Liam provides the soundtrack.

The Coconut Brothers, 1976.

Ruff in the jungle, St Lucia, 1994.

Leeroy and Liam filming an episode of *Get Stuffed*.

The Prodigy – Electronic Punks.

CHAPTER 7

"I wanted to make an album that really surprised people."

Liam

At the start of 1994, and with the difficult but highly successful transition step of 'One Love' under their belts, The Prodigy could now turn to their next album, which was due to be released in July of that year. For Liam, this would represent an intensely demanding challenge, because the previous album had consisted of tracks that the band had PA-ed and used for many months before the actual long player – now he was faced with producing a whole batch of brand new material from scratch. Liam's detailed description of the writing process for this second album offers a fascinating insight into the creative mind behind The Prodigy's music, and gives an opportunity to appreciate the level of integrity and skill

The Prodigy

involved in his work: "I wanted to make an album that really surprised people. As the year went on I bought a lot of albums and listened to loads of people for inspiration. Since I didn't go out as much now, and I wasn't getting as many ideas from our actual shows, most of my inspiration this time around was from records, and in particular non-dance music. So I wanted to surprise people and to touch a mark – for me the object of writing music is to touch an emotion. Whether it makes you feel happy or sad or whatever, it has to have a feeling. For example, I bought the new Beastie Boys album and that had a track on there with this fiddle all over it, and I was listening to that in the darkness of my room and it hit that mark. When I write I have to get that buzz, that tingle almost, and when I come up with a sound or a riff that has an effect on me then I know it's working. I wanted the whole album to have that effect. Music for me has to touch that mark."

Interestingly, Liam does not picture specific events or incidents when he is writing a track. Instead he prefers to focus on atmospheres and environments to inspire him: "I am inspired by scenes rather than events. Musically I try to set the scene for people. I used that methodology to create 'The Narcotic Suite', the three-song concept piece about the whole drugs scene at the end of the album. The first track of the set, 'Three Kilos' is a good example of that. When I was writing that, I pictured this smoky room with a load of laid-back people in there with this whole smoky vibe, and I could hear the music that went with that environment. Then the second track 'Skylined' had a whole up-lifting rush feel to it. The last track, 'Claustrophobic Sting', was inspired by visions of real paranoia, a 'depths of hell' track. In many senses, that particular track is the most forbidding I have ever written. It's heavy, very heavy and obliquely abstract. That whole piece was all pictures to me. When people say 'ambient' they think of the Aphex Twin and The Orb, real nice floaty sounds, but ambient is just music that creates atmospheres, music that is for a certain picture. Another example is the track 'Speedway' which is also very visual – the way it is programmed sounds as if these bikes are flying out at you, the sounds I have used create this picture, very visual. Quite a lot of the tracks on the second album were like that. In that sense I write like an ambient artist, I see pictures in my head, I am good at putting music to pictures. Mind you, there are various ways of writing and it is healthy to use them all at times. Take 'No Good (Start The Dance)' for example, that is just a real hard club song, it didn't set a picture other than a hard club. It wasn't a visual song, it was a simple song that had the right effect."

On this album, Liam experienced his most serious writing block to date – his productivity had always been high, with about 70% of the tracks that he started being used as finished pieces, but here he was struggling to get the initial spark, and found that he could not force the muse, and therefore had to take regular breaks from his work: "The album wasn't written over a solid six months. At first I went through a couple of experimental tracks but then dried up completely, and thought, 'Fuck, where am I going to get the rest of this album from?' So I forgot the whole project for a month and just spent a lot of time listening to loads of other music, snowboarding, going on holiday and gigging, including a great show at The Marquee in London. I got into all sorts of stuff, such as The Beastie Boys, Rage Against The Machine, Floyd, Senser, ambient, Ted Nugent, Deep Purple, getting loads of inspiration from stuff that was so far away from what I was used to writing. One of the most inspirational records I have from that period is the *Flash Gordon* soundtrack by Queen, which will probably sound really stupid. I don't like the single, 'Flash, ah-ha' and all that bollocks, but the rest of the album is amazing. I listened to that so many times and it inspired me so much. All the detail in there is incredible, and the little pieces of music are so brilliant, that is a real ambient album. After a month away from the actual recording I came back fresh with all these new ideas and influences spinning around in my head, and thereafter the material just flowed much easier. Furthermore, the break meant I avoided the pitfall of all the tracks sounding too similar to each other."

Once Liam had negotiated the writing block, he found that his own new material then became the influence for each subsequent track: "The actual first track that went down was 'Break and Enter'. All the time I was thinking 'This next track has to be different'. 'Voodoo People' for example, was me wanting to create a track that had no synth in there and was totally based on live segments. I had started listening to guitar music more around the time of 'One Love', but initially I never thought about incorporating it into our music. Once I had 'Voodoo People' completed, that pushed me on to a new writing approach because it was a really different sound, and with that in mind I drew inspiration out of my own track to write the next one, which was 'Their Law'. I took the track that Pop Will Eat Itself had sent me and chopped it up and got 'Their Law' based only on parts of the main riff. It has a real street sound, pure skateboard, surf guitars with heavy drums, real hardcore, elements of hip-hop and slow, heavy beats as well. 'Their Law' has so much aggression in it, it's totally hard. I really liked that sound, it had the feel and sound of a band song. In turn, that inspired me to push for more even variety on the next track, and so it progressed, with each new track inspiring me to write something else, giving me ideas for what the album was missing. I built the album up like that really, it almost wrote itself."

The danger of releasing an album with such a high degree of variety is that any composite coherence is lost in the process, and the project falls down by being too disparate. Liam was confident that he could avoid this and instead used the variety to his advantage: "Variety opens up another life for the band and that is what I wanted most from that record. I didn't care if people liked it or not, as long as it was varied. Essential to my creativity is the fact that with The Prodigy I don't feel tied to any one style of music, which would severely restrict me. If this second album had been the same as the first, all fast breakbeat hardcore, I would have been struggling, then I would have really worried about burning out from a lack of scope. Whereas all I care about now is writing music that I like. I am gradually expanding as I hear all these totally different styles, and that gives me so much more range. Within those aims, I still feel the record holds together as a coherent project. A track like 'Three Kilos' will totally surprise an original Prodigy fan, but in the context of the whole record it has its place. Every track on the album has its place."

Liam realises that progression has to be a gradual thing for any band and for this reason he was careful not to completely exclude the style that The Prodigy had become renowned for. At the same time, he mixed this with a few more experimental tracks, pushing the parameters out a little more with each tune: "The new album is half following on from before, whilst the other half is totally new. Some of the material I have never touched before, and there's also tracks that I touched way back when I was into hip-hop – for example 'Poison'. That is only 104 bpm which is really laid-back and far slower than I would have thought I would write, a real down-tempo track. I haven't written anything that slow since my hip-hop days. That track could lose us a lot of fans because it is so slow, but the point is that slow tracks can be the hardest tracks if they are written right. 'Poison' is proof of that school of thought, because despite its speed it is still one of the hardest tracks on the album. I wanted to bring Maxim into the picture a bit more and that track came together very well. He tried a few lyrical ideas but they weren't working, then he came back with the 'Poison' lyric which is not a rap or reggae or anything. I liked it, there were drug ambiguities in there as well, and as a result of the buzz that idea gave me, the track was finished very quickly. I really enjoyed writing it and it is a stand out track for me. It is a mix between hip-hop and techno and Maxim works perfect on there.

Ironically, that track is also perhaps the most autobiographical I have ever written. Hip-hop was the first style of music I was really into and that track has a lot of that element. It sums up that portion of my life well. Musically it represents the biggest chunk of my life I suppose, it is basically a hip-hop memory of all the stuff I was into before the band began. That is one of the key new tracks on the record and then interspersed with these new offerings are the tracks that you could say were inter-related with previous material, not exactly throwbacks, but moreover material that had more in common with the band's musical heritage. 'Break and Enter' is a good example. It had the feel of the rhythm section of 'Charly', the beats are similar, but slightly different. I suppose it's what I might have done if I had re-mixed a long version of 'Charly'. It's much longer though, a real build up but with the same flavour, a typical Prodigy tune but with a little bit more. Even if you are visiting familiar ground, you have to adapt and things should always move on."

When the second album was nearing completion, Liam was growing slowly more confident of its quality, and when it came to the cut, he had few reservations: "The only thing I regret is that I could have put a different version of 'One Love' on there, but there was just no time. I even had another track called 'We Eat Rhythm' when I arrived at the cutting room, because I didn't realise that you can only get 79 minutes of music on a CD, so we had to chop 'The Heat (The Energy)', edit 'One Love' and cut out the whole of the 'We Eat Rhythm' track. It was an instrumental piece that took me absolutely ages to complete, but I'm pretty sure that it wouldn't really have added anything substantial to the album, so that was cool." It is interesting to note that when Liam took the record to be cut, his A&R man Richard Russell (with whom he had developed a very strong musical relationship) had only heard three finished tracks. Liam's own sense of quality control and high standards meant that Richard was happy to give him that rare degree of freedom with his material.

One of the strongest elements of the record that developed over the course of its writing was the degree of musicality and musicianship, a factor that would surprise even the most loyal of Prodigy fans. Liam's desire to experiment with unusual chord progressions and unorthodox structures imbued his writing with an individuality that was highly distinctive, and one which he deliberately pursued: "I might spend a week messing around with a sound, as I am really into weird chord arrangements and chords progressions. I like to do the unexpected, and I guess that is where my technical training on the piano comes in handy, because I think I might be able to hear melodies and chords that other writers might not. If I have a bass line I will usually be able to hear a string line over that fairly quickly. On the other hand, it is crucial to remember that some tracks don't need to be musical at all, they need that random, yet programmed feel about them. Some of the techno tracks that come out can't really be written down musically, and there's nothing wrong with that."

Thematically, the record began to form around the abstract concept of the struggles of the generation that

Liam had been a part of, the people who were now being persecuted for their parties, for their way of life and for being something that the authorities could not understand. In calling the album *Music For The Jilted Generation*, Liam effectively wrote the soundtrack for the constant battle between the establishment and this disillusioned and substantial minority. Tracks like 'Break And Enter' and 'Speedway (Theme from Fastlane)' were sideswipes at the authority and in 'Their Law', the collaboration with Pop Will Eat Itself, the lead vocal of "fuck 'em and their law" made the most explicit and dismissive reference to the by-now controversial Criminal Justice Bill. Inadvertently, Liam had produced a highly politicised record, and that was yet more new territory for The Prodigy: "The track with PWEI is a good reference point. I have always said that we are not a political band, but this was just one point that could not go untouched, this whole law about partying is such bollocks. How any government can tell young people that they can't go out, these powers to search and disperse and all that bullshit. I wanted one track where that point was put across very directly, and although 'Their Law' is aggressive musically, I wanted to be able to put it across with more lyrics, much more vocally. It was essential to have that point made crystal clear. Over time, the album was forming a concept without me realising it – it was never meant to be an anti-Criminal Justice Bill album, but the way it was put together and the political events that developed around the time of the record meant that it was seen as much more political than we intended, which was totally by accident. There is a danger then of being seen as too blatant and too direct. We have always been anti-police, no-one in the band likes them or authority. Also, the sleeve of the record was exactly how we planned it, but it was not intended as a blatant anti-CJB piece, and now I am wary of being seen as a spokesperson. In a sense we represent the very opposite of that politicised stance, in that we are about good, hard dance music that people can listen to and forget all their troubles, forget politics and just enjoy themselves. That is all I want to do. 'The Jilted Generation' implication was a totally valid and genuine angle for the atmosphere to the second album, but at the same time I am still convinced that, ultimately, the actual buzz of the band is dance music not politics. I didn't have a whole politicised vision when I started, but in the end it shaped up pretty well. The whole album represents exactly what we are about."

Liam's own insight into the writing and development of the album offers detailed descriptions and sneaks of the creative world which he inhabits, but it is equally fascinating to hear the words of Neil McClellan, the producer of some tracks on the album, and thus far the only outsider who had *ever* had any musical input whatsoever into Liam's work. Liam had liked McClellan's work on N Joi's 'Adrenalin' EP and used him for production duties on 'One Love'. With the success of that track, it was then decided that the new album needed a similar degree of outside objectivity to fulfil its potential. As a man in a unique position to observe Liam at work, Neil has seen what no-one else has – the nucleus of his creative process: "I thought his previous recorded output had been brilliant, but I sensed that Liam was straining at the leash, that he wanted to go deeper and heavier. Once he came to the studios, my suspicions were confirmed, and very quickly I realised I was dealing with a unique writer. His approach is a really bizarre writing method and I have never seen anyone else who writes music in the same way that Liam does. He hasn't got an amazing knowledge of the gear he is using – of course he knows what it all does, but he has this unique approach that totally blows you away when you first see it. It's not even that he uses state-of-the-art gear, a Roland W30 is something that you buy as your first piece of gear, real lo-tech, but that makes absolutely no difference. I had to check out the water for the first two hours, so I just rolled a spliff and sat back whilst we were setting up the gear and listening to these tracks he had already done at home. I was just totally blown away. The music was so impressive. I would listen to a track and think, 'Wouldn't it be great if there was a high string phrase in here' and then in the next bar there would be, Liam had thought of everything. Then when I saw how he actually worked, it was incredible, the process was such a very fast one. It might take him a while to actually write the track, but once he has the ideas fixed in his mind it is a very fast process indeed. He plays everything in manually, rather than looping sections all the time, it's amazing to watch, and can be so fast. I just stood aside and watched as he made this outrageous music so quickly, with no messing about. I have worked on a lot of computer music but never anything like Liam's."

McClellan was also impressed with Liam's use of samples, a skill that poorer dance music so often abuses:

The Prodigy

"Some of the ideas he has for samples are so obscure and yet so well known – he digs really deep for them. He takes a sample and chops it up incredibly fine, sometimes into 16th notes and then uses that in such a strange and unique way. The point to remember is this: it is really easy to write bad electronic music, because anyone can sit in front of a computer, but to write good electronic music is very, very difficult. Liam does that. One of the reasons he can do this is because he is harder against himself than he is against anyone else, his personal quality control and musical attention to detail is meticulous. If there is even a slight inkling of doubt then an idea is thrown out. As a human being he takes no shit and absolutely drives himself hard, and that manifests itself in the music and his prolific nature. When I worked with him that attitude made me totally conscious of the amount I was putting in, and consequently I made sure I was working at least as hard as him, so I think we drove each other into the ground. With Liam, you can't mess about, he expects absolute professionalism – in many studio environments there are all sorts of vices and distractions flying around, but Liam will have none of it. He is so single-minded, I have never seen anything like it."

There was also a highly experimental attitude to the actual recording process, which to McClellan was like a breath of fresh air: "Liam seems to do things differently every time he starts a new track. For example, many people take a sample and tune all the keyboards to that, but Liam will do quite the opposite and fit all the keyboards to the sample. He will get the sample sounding exactly right and then tune all the keyboards down to that, so none of the equipment is really in the key that it says it is. To say how he does that or where he gets the inspiration from is impossible, because he does things differently every time, and always totally from instinct. I loved that element, because you can make the best and hardest dance music in that way. Take the didgeridoo sound on 'One Love' for example – that was made by Liam wah-wahing and me messing around with the EQ. We got other sounds by trying all sorts of mad things. For example, we put a speaker underneath a grand piano playing a 303 bassline, taped up all the piano strings and then put an effects box in there as well which created an inhuman amount of feedback, a really bizarre sound. Another example of the recording innovation was when we put a brick on the piano's sustain pedal, so that all the strings were just above the hammer and then we fed the effects unit through there again. Also, Liam's use of guitars was absolutely brilliant, and the heavy crass beats over those guitars were superb. All the things that you are traditionally supposed to keep quiet in a studio, we just cranked up as much as possible. Liam was totally open to ideas but all the time was also very aware of what was and wasn't working. It was so enjoyable, doing things I have always wanted to try, because Liam gives you as much room as you want. That degree of innovation is a natural and instinctive creative talent, it can't be learnt and it's just incredible to watch someone that naturally gifted at work."

Once the album was finished McClellan was taken aback by the composite result and views the project with obvious reverence: "There is nothing on that album that I would say I didn't like and would want to change, and that is very, very rare for a producer to say. The second album is far superior to the first. *Experience* struggled to appeal to anyone other than rave kids, but having said that as a time-piece it was excellent. It was linear in that sense, a narrow spectrum of appeal. It still had the melodies, despite some of the beats sounding dated now, the melodies were very strong. One thing you should notice about Liam's music is that no matter what else is going on, there is always a melody line, something that hooks you and you will go away humming, and that is not as easy as people think to achieve. This new record by comparison was so totally innovative, I knew there was *nothing* else out there that sounded remotely like it. His writing had even progressed noticeably from 'One Love' to some of the hip-hop tracks on the album. There is so much variety on there. As a recording process. it was completely unorthodox. I have worked on a lot of stuff, and no matter how experimental the work appears to be at first, somewhere along the line an orthodoxy will develop, a traditional structure or methodology which you can recognise will creep in, but that never happened with Liam. In that sense there is nothing traditional about his work – I haven't seen anyone else write music like he does. Seeing him work on that album just blew me away."

★   ★   ★

The first release after this intensive spell of writing came in the form of The Prodigy's eighth single, entitled 'No

Good (Start The Dance)'. It was a track that had been played in their usual testing ground at PAs for over eight months now, where it was received very well. Over that period it had taken on various forms, and the final mix for the single represented a few problems for Liam. The original version, called simply 'Start The Dance', was 150bpm, a hard techno track. Then he slowed it down to 130bpm for a US mix but was not happy with the result and so returned it to its original pace. However, he was still not convinced that the record had the hook and the core feature that singles need, and so after much deliberation he decided to place a female vocal over the music as the lead line. The decision played heavily on his mind and he is still not entirely comfortable with the move, despite the single's subsequent success: "I almost felt like I had let myself down by putting that female vocal on it. It was such a fine line, and I wasn't sure if it worked or not. If I think something is no good musically but will sell, I absolutely will not use it. It's a fine line though between what works and what sells, and with 'Start The Dance' there was a doubt in my mind, it was almost *too* catchy to use. The same happened with 'Out Of Space', but at the time there were a lot of similar things around. Every time I write a tune I am wary of falling into any category and the female vocal on 'Start The Dance' was a brave move because we could have been dissed for having an obvious female vocal in there. All that poppy European female techno shit is worthless and we managed to avoid being grouped in with that, but as far as catchy vocals go, 'Start The Dance' is the last track I will release with that on it. You can be a lot more creative than that with vocals. Still, it was a hard club tune and for the context it was written and the ideas I had in my head during its development, I think it worked quite well."

The record buying public agreed with him – the single reached No.4 in the charts and stayed in the Top 10 for seven weeks, in the process selling in excess of 250,000 copies. The beats and bass were as hard as ever, but there was more musicality here, more sophistication, and the frenetic groove was made all the more impressive because of this greater integrity. The coruscating rhythm was cleverly injected with enough space and melody to make a good, hard, street-level track. Once again the B-side offered more glimpses into Liam's mad world, with extensive remixes by CJ Bolland and David Morley that offered virtually complete new tracks (this is a practice that Liam deliberately pursues) – it all made for a very powerful release. In some ways it was a more traditional Prodigy release than 'One Love', but that did not mean that the band remained stationery with this record. Whereas 'One Love' had broken the band into new musical territory and opened up whole new horizons for the sonic landscape of The Prodigy, 'No Good' completed the transition by breaking into new visual areas and angles for the band's representation. It did this in one very simple step – with the band's best video so far.

In the video, the band enter a neglected and disused underground warehouse where a relatively low-key party is taking place, and wander around the rooms lingering at various points to take in what they see. After a while, they head off in search of their own corners of the party where they each let off steam in whichever way suits best. Keith, although initially quite mellow, soon becomes insane and unstable, whilst Leeroy finds an empty room and starts a dance frenzy. Liam watches quietly for a long while before smashing up a brick wall whilst Maxim, complete with cat's eyes, just sits and observes the whole proceedings. With the band being filmed in slow motion whilst the rest of the actors are in normal speed, and with the film being shot in colour then drained to black and white, the overall grainy effect is very much of a dark, seedy, gangster world inhabited by both the strange and the normal with a sinister, pervading sense of heavy paranoia. It was aggressive, angry, and very hard, the absolute visual reflection of the track itself. The video was a breakthrough for the band in one key way – for the first time the camera dwells on each individual band member for lengthy periods of time, allowing the viewer to focus on them and begin to assimilate some perception of each identifiable character and personality. Until now, The Prodigy's videos (and indeed the majority of those in the hard dance genre) were flash shots of band members switching quickly from frame to frame with little chance to see the actual faces and characters. With this excellent promo, The Prodigy made their first concessions to the public desire to see what they looked and acted like, a concession which will always be dichotomous with the band's own desire to avoid becoming stars in any way. At the same time, they took a serious step towards silencing the by-now rather tedious and reactionary criticism that all proponents of techno and its various musical families were faceless acts. The new director of the band's videos was Walter Stern, and he appeared to be in touch with exactly what the band wanted to portray. He found a disused market cellar beneath Spitalfields in the East End of London, and concentrated on giving the film a street-level, hard look, something in his words which was "real and normal yet weird, like the party scene in *Jacob's Ladder*."

The video received heavy rotation on MTV and consequently the singles sales maintained a healthy high, hence the long chart life. In addition, this exposure on Europe's premier music channel introduced The Prodigy to millions of new listeners, and established them as a band with their own independent identity. The original version of the video had to be cut so that the 'scenes of distress' that MTV will not show were removed, but fortunately this did not lessen the impressive impact of the promo. This heavy air play was a first for the band; although 'One Love' had been played, this was the first time any video of theirs had been used so much – the video was still being played three months after the single had finally dropped out of the charts. In doing this, the band picked up a much more varied and wider fan-base, which coincided with their increased number of college and European dates that came with this higher profile abroad. The visual progress of 'No Good (Start The Dance)' now complemented the musical evolution of the previous single, which combined together to increase the already high expectations for the release of the forthcoming second album, *Music For The Jilted Generation* album. Even so, nobody could have expected just what The Prodigy were about to unleash on the nation's ears.

CHAPTER 8

*"So, I've decided to take my work back
underground, to stop it falling
into the wrong hands."*

And so begins The Prodigy's second album, *Music For The Jilted Generation* – it was not a sample that was chosen lightly. After all the difficulties and misinterpretations that the band had continually endured, this was an immediate statement of intent, a withdrawal from the fame game back into the underground from whence they had come. The clicking typewriter and weary hushed voice which delivers this opening line leads the listener into a propulsive modern dance record, an otherworldly opus with layer upon layer of fractious patterns, supremely organised hooks, arrangements, dynamics, bridges and breakdowns all building into an immense pitch of tension and emotion, which unlike the first singular album, was much more accumulative in nature. *Jilted Generation* was a complex, mutated alchemy of moods, and a very serious piece of music indeed. Beginning with the full speed and ammoral ambiguity of 'Break and Enter', the album scorched through a series of dynamics, slowing down for the brooding metal of 'Their Law', peaking again with the breathtaking 'Speedway (Theme From Fastlane)', dipping again with the lysergic anthemic minimalism of 'One Love' before speeding up once more for the cavernous collage of 'Full Throttle', before culminating in the highly disturbing 'Narcotic Suite' with its cataclysmic death throes of 'Claustrophobic Sting'. There was heavy breakbeat speeding with 'Full Throttle', set in direct contrast to the jazz funky grooves of '3 Kilos'. The much heralded use of guitars produced one of the album highlights in the maniacal 'Voodoo People', arguably the finest example to date of the collision between techno and rock, and a concrete confirmation of the scope of The Prodigy's new vision. There was a return to hip-hop with the crushingly hard beats of 'Poison' and a straight hard dance track in 'No Good (Start The Dance)'. With the closing concept piece 'Narcotic Suite', the sonic journey is finished in a musical room filled with drug experiences, with each mood being communicated by the three tracks, where the orchestral brooding of 'Skylined' pre-empts 'Claustrophobic Sting' which was one of the most unsettling and clinically disorientating final tracks of recent years. Throughout the record, the sampled dialogue and twisted snatches of voices hint at a range of moods and ideas, a palate of emotion spliced with subtle anti-social polemic. The degree and complexity of sonic detail hides the delicacy of the production and writing, without brutalising the record into submission. Perhaps the finest (and rarest) achievement here was that the record was instantly identifiable as The Prodigy, despite the fact that it was a cauldron of sound and extreme variety – far from being faceless and too clinical, this had a distinct and specific identity. The record was a dark offering and a huge stylistic jump from the more linear and celebratory *Experience*. This was highly sophisticated and yet very direct – the result was an overwhelming headrush of hard music, an expression of aural hedonism which as a composite provided one of the most notable hard dance records ever written.

Interestingly, Liam kept much of the album from the band, keeping his work relatively under wraps compared to previous releases. So when they heard the composite for the first time, their reaction was understandably strong, and is probably best summed up by Keith, who said: "I am probably the biggest pessimist of the band, always wary, always cautious, but when I heard that album I thought, 'Fucking hell, I am connected to this incredible record, I am a part of this'. That was such a buzz, I knew it was an amazing record from the second I heard it. It was such a progression. I went round Liam's house three or four times and said, 'Sorry to bother you again Liam, but I've just listened to that album again and you are a genius!' I just couldn't believe it, and the fact that I was connected to it. I knew it would do well because there is so much variety on there." Leeroy was even more taken aback: "I think me, Keith and Maxim are the luckiest bastards in the world, 'cos we get to hear all this shit before anyone else, and we get that buzz first. Liam just does something with the music that is unbelievable. He is a perfectionist and that shows, it is consistently high quality original stuff. There are other good bands and good records out there, but the shit he does is fantastic, no-one can get near him."

Having said all this, when The Prodigy prepared to release the album, they were still receiving almost no mainstream radio airplay, limited television other than MTV, almost no documentation and support from the media, and repeated and continual derogatory reviews from their own genre. So it was all the more impressive when the record entered the National album charts at No.1 and outsold the rest of the Top 3 put together. In the week of its release, the album sold three times more than its nearest competitor. The only challenger to its place at the top was the release the following week of The Rolling Stones' first album in five years, but The Prodigy's record went on to stay in the charts for longer than even this, with the record still being in the Top 20 four months after its release. The accolades came flooding in – within a week it had passed the 60,000 mark (silver), 100,000 (gold) within two more and it then exceeded sales of *Experience* in only two months. Overseas sales were high as well for the first time, particularly in Germany, but also in Israel, Greece, and Benelux; this was a substantial improvement on the success of *Experience* which never broke heavily into territories other than the UK, since its linear breakbeat form was something that had a particularly British appeal and colloquial sound. The result of all this recognition was that the album's hefty immediate sales figures continued and shot past the half a million mark in less than five months.

Previous to this release, The Prodigy, and indeed most other alternative dance bands, had been given little or no coverage in the music press – it was only as 1994 arrived and this genre continued to produce quality material that this started to change. Even then however, acts like Aphex Twin and Orbital still received more respect and serious attention than The Prodigy, as the trend of suspicion and discredit continued against the band. For this reason, it is interesting to highlight for a moment the ecstatic press reaction to this record, bearing in mind this previous history of indifference and criticism. *NME* was unreserved in its praise and said, "At 23, Liam Howlett is a complete pop genius" and "a Robocop and a modern-day Beethoven rolled into one," and also went on to say that The Prodigy were "the most important rock and roll band of the 1990s". The general response was that in *Jilted Generation* Liam had produced a work of genius, that he had completed his transformation from an underground cult to a respected and revered writer of highly innovative music. In terms of how they were treated in the press, it was quite a turn around but one which, to their credit, the media were not ashamed to admit.

The one worrying reaction from the press was the emphasis they placed on the political elements of the album. True, it was written by someone deeply immersed in his generation's conflagration with authority, and was therefore, by definition, both a political and highly contemporary statement. Also true was the fact that The Prodigy themselves had been taken offstage several times by the police, both before and after they had become commercially successful. Furthermore, the artwork for the album clearly portrayed the exact style of confrontation that was taking place up and down the country. In addition, the album arguably espoused a criminal undertone, with echoes of joyriding, burglary, drugs and high-speed racing. All these factors justifiably caused people to focus on the politics of the album, and place it in the extraneous circumstances and socio-political environment it was released in, as the perfect answer to the Criminal Justice Bill and the authorities in general. Developments around the CJB had accelerated throughout 1994 and the summer season saw demonstrations and even small riots against its introduction. This coincided with *Jilted Generation* being at its peak, and hence it became a soundtrack to the unrest and discontent of a whole body of disenfranchised and angry people. All these factors are undeniable.

However, the band were uneasy with the increasing focus placed on this socio-political angle. As a result of this enforced political emphasis, they were now faced with a dilemma of sorts – if they renounced their argument they would be both untrue to themselves and also hypocritical to the public; at the same time, if they pursued the anti-CJB angle and hammered home their views, they were in grave danger of being seen as spokesmen and figureheads for the movement. In many senses, this was exactly the same situation that they had been threatened with when magazines were featuring them as 'Rave's Last Hope' and other such absurd headlines – once again The Prodigy found themselves at the centre of a very delicate situation in terms of how they wished to be perceived. So, in interviews the band tried to emphasis they were in fact still a dance band, and that this was ultimately why they existed – to make people dance. This course of action was not pre-emptive however, and coming as it did after the chain of events had already taken matters out of their hands to a certain degree, the band would have to wait to see if the political emphasis placed on their album by other people would prove to be a future millstone around their necks.

The press did not see this element as a flaw however – far from it, and their acclaim was such that *Jilted Generation* was nominated for the prestigious Mercury Music Award. Also amongst the ten nominees were Blur, M People, Pulp, Ian McNabb, Take That, Therapy?, Paul Weller, Shara Nelson and Michael Nyman. The nomination itself was a recognition of the impact of *Jilted Generation* and the band were 8-to-1 third favourites to win behind Blur and M People (the eventual winners). Also of note was the fact that when Susie Fletcher, a top MTV executive, was asked which album she thought should win, without hesitation she announced *Jilted Generation*. The Prodigy album was comfortably the most inventive record on offer, and as the panel themselves noted, was also the least derivative. Whilst the other nine bands scoured the history of music for inspiration, reflecting past glories, The Prodigy represented a genre that was perhaps the only genuinely new and totally innovative form of music in the 1990s. They were also the only band on show who had never won mainstream radio airplay. At the formal award ceremony, the band awkwardly milled around avoiding the tuxedo-clad executives and high-powered cameras, and when they collected their award for the nomination, they politely pointed out that although they were pleased, this was not the reason why they actually made their music. The main highlight of the night was when they gave an interview for radio to a man who clearly knew absolutely nothing about the band. They spent fifteen minutes telling him they were actually a grunge band from Seattle called The Pythons, who had come to the UK on tour, but had been so overwhelmed by the power of rave and techno that they had immediately changed styles completely and moved wholesale to the UK. The DJ taped everything and then trundled off to his studio to broadcast the interview word for word, with the band's sniggers following him down the corridor.

There was one major disappointment and failure at this time – the collapse of the band's American record deal. Since signing to Elektra, the group had enjoyed only very minor success in the States, with the *Experience* album selling just 70,000 copies, which in that market was very poor, almost negligible. The difficulties with the American tour – administratively and with their health – had complicated matters and slowed progress down even further, since the band had not returned to gig over there since those stressful days. The Prodigy then became concerned when Elektra continually requested more palatable remixes of the tracks that were being released in the UK, saying the original versions were too extreme for the American market. This attitude became all the more confusing when the record company then refused to release 'One Love' at all in the States, saying it was unsuitable, despite the fact that it was The Prodigy's least hardcore and perhaps most accessible track to date. Elektra seemed both unsure of how to market the band and unconvinced of their potential. The situation was not ideal and the result was that Elektra dropped The Prodigy less than a month after *Jilted Generation* had stormed to the top of the British charts.

★   ★   ★

In a year when The Prodigy enjoyed the huge success of their second album, they could perhaps have been forgiven for taking things a little easier on the gig front – not so, in 1994 they played a show every four days, taking in 25 countries and being watched by over 300,000 people. With the album's success reaching such heights, there was a notable shift in gear in both the numbers attending the shows and the nature of the gigs they were playing. The move from the dance circuit-only venues had been started the previous year and was now implemented in earnest, with the band visiting arenas and festivals that were traditionally associated with guitar and rock music. Also, the increased number of overseas gigs was continued, not to avoid over-exposure in the UK but simply to service all the new territories which had latched onto the band as a result of the international success of the second album. It was a sign of the band's newly-gained fan-base that they could not only play these international festival circuit dates, but in some cases headline them. The tour kicked off early in preparation for the forthcoming album, with shows in Holland and Australia, before officially commencing the album support back in Britain for a ten-date run, culminating with the band's headline slot at the enormous 35,000 capacity Feile Festival. This was just the first of many festivals that the band were to play in the summer of 1994, and they found the experience very different from the smaller venues they were used to. The sheer scale of the gigs meant that the buzz of the crowd was based more on the numbers and much less on actual personal contact. In July, the band played to over 150,000 people in one five-festival spell alone. In addition, the band found themselves on the same bill as bands such as The Red Hot Chili Peppers and Biohazard, which gave them yet more new material and hard live shows to learn from – the band agreed that the Chili Peppers performance was one of the greatest gigs they had ever seen. By the second stage of a two-part British tour for the album which came in October, the band had succeeded in making this substantial step up to the echelon of bands capable of playing arenas, and the result was that this second tour was sold out completely one month in advance. So much for dance bands not being able to play live.

Whilst The Prodigy were on tour promoting their smash album, they also released their ninth single, 'Voodoo People', a track which instantly took hard dance music into a whole new territory with its excellent and uncompromising marriage of rock guitars, fast tribal rhythms, mad flutes and infectious vocal backdrop. Once again the Dust Brothers remixes on the B-side received warm acclaim, but it was Liam's dynamic lead track that took all the honours – with this single the genuine pioneering element of the band was now in full swing. The video was another stylistic progression for the band, and continued the personality-based presentation that had been developing since the 'No Good' promo. The scene was a tropical island (St. Lucia in fact) and Liam, Maxim and Keith were all being pursued by Leeroy, who was a voodoo witch doctor. The video contained some genuine scenes of authentic voodoo which the band had to carefully research because of the nature of the occult, and there were scenes of human torture and rituals which eventually had to be cut from the MTV version to exclude the 'scenes of distress' once more. The music channel still gave it heavy rotation, and with the release entering the charts at No.11, it confirmed that The Prodigy had successfully negotiated their crucial transitional phase.

With 'Voodoo People' riding high in the charts, The Prodigy continued with their relentless schedule. On this tour, the two-fold nature of The Prodigy was even more accentuated – there are the records and the live shows, and both offer a totally different experience. Now the act onstage was more theatrical, with Keith thrashing around in a straitjacket or being locked in a smoke-filled glass box, frantically trying to escape. Other times, Maxim took a more overt role, with the band's first lyrical involvement live for the hard hip-hop of 'Poison'. Leeroy was even more hyperactive, and by now his dance routines had become highly revered. At the back of all this was Liam, the sorcerer of the musical mayhem that causes all the madness in front of him, lunging at his mass of gear inside a metal frame. Above him hung a screen that flashed between random psychedelic images to shots from the back of the stage, showing The Prodigy's stage craft up close. The band's evolving vision was furthered with the entrance of a guitarist onstage for some tracks, a development that was met with surprising enthusiasm by the crowd. The light show became an extravaganza, with the stage being hemmed in by two more screens flickering with scatterings of hi-tech imagery, and the whole combined effect was like watching a mass hysteria of band and public, with only the band seeming to be in control of the dementia.

Their antics on the road continued with as much chaos as the live show, accompanied all the time with the regular band wager of £50 for the most obscene Polaroid taken. In Switzerland, the band were driving to the next show after a successful performance in Zurich, when they started to climb a steep incline that cut into the side of a snow-capped mountain, with the sounds of Snoop Doggy Dog's tune 'Suicide' thumping out of the tour bus stereo. Just as the band were really getting into the track, the bus stopped and started to slow down, then to their horror it began sliding backwards on the black ice, heading straight for the precipice of the 300-foot mountain, over which was a sheer drop into the blackness below. For what seemed like hours the bus slid nearer and nearer, all the time with the lyrics screaming out in the background "suicide, it's a suicide", whilst the band clutched the seats with white knuckles and prepared for the quickest descent of a mountain they had ever made.

Fortunately, just five metres from the edge the bus started to grip the road, and then hit a small post which finally and thankfully brought it to rest. Nervous laughs and false bravado chuckled around the bus before they moved on again, this time with something a little less ominous on the stereo.

In Holland, Liam and Keith set out on their first press-only tour, which consisted of a week of interviews, radio slots and other media work, with no gigs at all. These promotional tours are dreaded by most musicians, but this time Liam had a severe cold and was suffering from bouts of nausea and dizziness which made the prospect even less welcoming. After only a day of inane interviews, filled with questions like, "Yes, but you don't all play instruments, so is this real music?" Liam announced that due to his ill health he could do no more, and that he wanted to cancel all the remaining interviews and go home. His press officer persuaded him that this was not in anyone's interests, and eventually a compromise was reached – he would complete the week's work in bed, and the journalists would have to come to him instead. Arrangements were hurriedly made and so Liam and Keith lay back in bed for three days, with suitable provisions, whilst a continent of writers filed past, asked a barrage of often stupid questions, and then filed out. Keith found the whole week a blast: "We were absolutely stoned on skunk the whole time, and it became a surreal experience in the end, because we lost track of which interview was which. We had the porno channel on, plates full of cakes and drinks, and weed all over the place. We just interviewed one, then shouted 'next' all week. One guy who came in was a spit of Jimi Hendrix, and after that amount of weed it was all a little strange." Keith's preference for a smoke sent him to sleep on one occasion midway through an interview, whereupon he dozed off for what he thought was a few minutes, then woke with a start and said, "Right, where were we?" He had actually been slumbering for three hours and Liam had trawled his way through the next nine interviews.

The band's interaction with the audience did not always go to plan. In Newcastle, Maxim watched as one fan managed to fight his way through the hordes of swarming fans, drag himself up on to the barrier, jump across the gap and negotiate his way past the angry and burly security guards before arriving finally on stage. Impressed by his determined endeavours, Maxim acknowledged him and started to chat some lines in his direction, but the fan was waving wildly to get his attention, pointing at his ears and shouting, "It's too loud, it's too loud, it's too loud!" At another show Maxim climbed to the top of a tall speaker and turned his back on the crowd, before falling backwards into what he thought would be a bed of welcoming arms. What he couldn't see was that, in the meantime, the audience had parted like the Red Sea and therefore stood and watched as the MC crashed to the floor in an untidy heap. Their amusement was increased at the end of the show when Liam coolly walked to the front of the crowd to shake someone's hand and promptly fell straight through a hole at the edge of the stage.

However, it was left to Keith to perform the most memorable stage-dive of the tour, a night which saw him pioneer a new style of laser show the like of which had never been seen before. As is his want, he frequently plunges into the crowd, glaring at them and spitting water over the nearest unfortunates, before being carried across a sea of hands around the venue and back to the stage. On this particular occasion, he dived into the crowd and found his shirt had been half-ripped off his back, about which he said, "All my gut was hanging out and I'm hardly Take That, so I can't really get away with it. Anyway, I was determined to try again, so I hauled myself back onstage and started again." This time he climbed over the monitors right to the edge of the stage and prepared himself once more for the dive about to come. Just as Keith leaped off, the burly security guard took exception to this, reached out his trunk-like arm and grabbed Keith's trousers' and boxer shorts' hem in one iron-fisted grip. Unfortunately, Keith's momentum was already too great to stop him falling forward, despite the attention of the guard, and the result was that his trousers and boxers were pulled right down to his ankles, whilst his lilly white Essex arse remained pointing skyward, in full view of the audience. Until the guard managed to regain his balance, the crowd was treated to a bewildering and world-first light show, as the hi-tech lasers and strobes bounced off Keith's protruding cheeks and lit up the venue, whilst in the background his hysterical friends tried to continue their performance despite their aching sides and the tears rolling down their faces.

A couple of shows later, the band were playing a large college and found their dressing room in the main metalwork classroom, where they were stuck amidst a motley collection of children's scooters (the old-fashioned two-wheel platform style with the long handle at the front), which were being made for the students' final exams. After entertaining themselves with these contraptions for ten minutes, the door opened and a local fan, completely off his head on acid, walked in and introduced himself to the band. They sat him down and proceeded to tell him that scooters were in fact the latest addition to their ever developing live show, and that to ride on of these was *the* hardest thing you could do on the underground club circuit in London. "Never mind drugs, snow boarding, body piercing and tattoos," said Liam, "this is where it's at, scooters, man". The fan just sat there amazed, taking this all in. Ten minutes before the show was to start, the band realised that they had no-one to introduce them onstage. Keith took the unsuspecting fan to one side and said, "You introduce us tonight, there's only a small crowd, maybe a couple of hundred, and this could be your big moment, this is your fifteen minutes of fame, right here and now." To the fan's drug-addled brain, Keith's encouragement that he was about to go down in rock history was completely convincing. What the band neglected to tell him however, was that the audience that night was actually well in excess of 3500 people. They ushered him to the side of the stage and as the lights went down he walked out on to the boards and was met by the massive roar of packed auditorium, but he just stood there, dazed and shaking, looking at the 3500 faces waiting for him to speak. After a pause of half a minute or so, during which time the sweat poured profusely from his forehead, he started to twitch and then finally spoke, and from his mouth came only "Wooooooaaaarrrrgg!! Gggggghhhhhhhhhhhh!!" over and over again, a torrent of utterly incomprehensible verbal spewing, that to his befuddled head meant, "Hello Ladies and Gentleman, please welcome onstage The Prodigy". The band spent the first two tracks of the show trying to stop laughing. Backstage after the show, they were delighted to see their friend waiting for them, and he was completely elated with his legendary performance. They filled his jacket pockets with cans of beer and bags of weed, then as a last gesture of appreciation Liam stood up, shook his hand and said, "Look man, that was the bollocks, the best introduction we've ever had. We'd like you to accept this scooter as a token of our gratitude." The fan could not believe it, it was all too much and at first he would not accept the gift. Finally he gratefully accepted, whereupon he headed off home with the biggest beaming smile across his face, and someone's beloved and precious hand-made scooter under his arm.

In Iceland the band were met by their first ever mob of fans at the airport, before driving on to the night's show in Reykjavik, in front of 4,000 fans. This size of crowd is impressive enough in the UK, but in Iceland it represented just over 1.5% of the entire population. As the band walked through the airport customs, the guard stopped Keith, took him to one side and said, "Do you have to take drugs to do your job?" to which Keith cheekily replied, "No, but I would if I had your job!" At the actual show, Maxim dived into the crowd and

The Prodigy

danced for a while, but found that when he was due to return to the stage, the over-zealous security men didn't recognise him and refused to let him get back – he eventually had to show them his backstage pass and microphone before they finally relented. Meanwhile, Liam realised half an hour into his set that his main piece of equipment had broken down, and he was left for the rest of the show having to play everything live, including drums, bass, lead lines and samples. Even so, the response was great and the difficult circumstances made for a good buzz. For Keith, who is regularly accused of taking drugs to perform as he does, this show was yet another case of vomiting before and during the show, such was the adrenalin inside him, something which happens at least 50% of the time: "I know it's been said before and it can sound clichéd, but the gig *is* a drug, a pure drug, you just don't need anything else. The performance is the narcotic."

In Japan, the band were to play two shows, one a commercial rave style event, and the other a more credible underground gig. When they arrived at their destination, the band were dismayed to see just how commercial and mainstream the first night was to be – they were on the same bill as pop acts like Cappella and 2 Unlimited. That night they all hit the town and at a record company party managed to drink over £300 worth of tequila between the four of them. With the band all suitably lubricated, they went out on to the streets to see the sights, where Maxim spotted an alley full of Japanese people breakdancing to some hard hip-hop tunes. Whilst his friends prepared to run for cover, Maxim casually walked over to the crew, picked the biggest one who was dancing, looked him up and down for his style and said, "I'll burn you, man". After drunkenly dancing with his new-found friends for a while, Maxim then spotted a passing dustcart and promptly jumped onto it and vanished into the night. Meanwhile, an equally inebriated Keith and Liam had gone in search of food, and had found a general store that looked ideal. Unfortunately, all of the packaging was obviously in Japanese, so Keith decided to open everything and try it first, "because I didn't want to go home with a box of tampons for my supper". The owner of the store watched as they trashed shelves full of goods, and then for some unknown reason Keith had a brilliant idea – he wanted to photocopy his arse. Liam helped him onto the store's machine and ran off a copy – the tone was too dark, so Keith politely asked the owner if he could help. Admirably, the owner came over and showed them how to work the machine, giving them tips on how to enlarge and reduce the Xeroxed arse, before returning a little later to see how they were getting on and to ask if they needed any more change.

★   ★   ★

Music For The Jilted Generation achieved much more than just heavy sales and award nominations. It announced that The Prodigy's musical parameters were now infinite, that they were a band of continual evolution and change, and it finally silenced their many detractors with its maturity and development – rave was now nothing more than a four-letter word. Perhaps one of the album's greatest achievements was the fact that it forced the industry to finally recognise The Prodigy, a band that had been ignored, snubbed and derided since its inception, regarded with a mixture of loathing, dread and condescension. With *Jilted Generation* being The Prodigy's sign that they were only just flexing their creative muscles, the possibilities for the band now were seemingly endless.

The Prodigy's music is hard, street level dance music, but their spirit and ethos is very much immersed in the punk spirit. This can be seen in a whole host of areas even − or especially − during these early years. Their success had been founded on music that was largely unpalatable to the mainstream and had been strongly complemented by exhaustive gig schedules, even after they enjoyed chart-topping album success. They had never rehearsed (but for that one failed attempt), so their live show was a spontaneous feast of improvisation and energy. Liam writes his music for himself, not to sell records, but to expand the vision of the band, with an integrity that is obliviously unconcerned with the commercial repercussions of such experimentalism. Furthermore, his writing and recording process at this early stage of their career was devoid of the mega-buck complications of protracted and extraneous studio involvements, with Liam effectively completing the entire process himself, save for a few guiding hands towards the finishing line. In addition, he continually refused to accept the proffered role as one of dance music's aristocrats. The music itself was effective without all the pseudo-analytical pretension that surrounded so much of contemporary music – it spoke directly to the body and contained as much soul and life as any of its peers, as well as incorporating a legion of other forms such as reggae, rap, rock, classical, punk, world beats, and funk, all with consummate ease. At the same time, The Prodigy were involved in a genre that did not drag its feet in the glories of yesteryear, but instead forged ahead with innovation as its guiding light.

Their consistent and repeated refusal to enter the mainstream media circus cost them at times during these early years, but they had no hesitation in continuing this approach of underselling – the mainstream had always been distasteful to the band and remains so to this day. Throughout their existence, The Prodigy have balanced street credibility with huge commercial success, a dichotomy that eludes all but the very sharpest of bands – despite selling in excess of three million records worldwide by the end of 1994, they only felt truly at home in the underground. This tenet extended to their own celebrity, or rather their determined efforts to avoid anything as such, and they manoeuvred around the 'faceless' accusations whilst not plunging into the theatricality of the fame game with a creditable degree of foresight. Their band control remained strong throughout their early career: even when they wore costumes, they designed the clothes themselves; since their inception they have dictated their image and presentation both in promotions, videos and on stage.

Their political involvement, although perhaps over-emphasised by the media, showed that they were a band operating on the very edge of contemporary events and

The Prodigy

underground culture. They matched their considerable popularity with an astute awareness of the vagaries of fashion and the fickle nature of the monolithic beast that is pop, and refused to make concessions to either. They did not confuse commercialism with success. They were outsiders, underdogs, interlopers, and misfits. Back then, in those exhilerating, frantic early days, The Prodigy were indeed electronic punks.

APPENDIX

The following interview is extracted from the book *The Right To Imagination & Madness*, originally published by IMP in 1994. The interview was conducted at Mike Champion's house in Essex in April of that year. Liam had just got back from a series of exhausting overseas dates and due to delayed flights had barely had a chance to unpack his suitcase; he declined my offer to rearrange, saying he didn't want to let me down.

MR: How did you begin in music?
LH: I've always been into stuff that is music on a street level, kind of underground. Initially, the first music I was into was ska. My dad bought me this tape of The Specials and Bad Manners, when they were still quite underground. Then I moved on to rap, Public Enemy's first album, the Ultra Magnetic MC's from New York, but not just the music, I was also into that whole scene, the graffiti, the scratching, the DJ-ing, the breakdancing thing, the mixing, everything. That was when I first took real notice of the actual music and started writing. The whole hip-hop scene was built up around the breakbeat thing so I got myself a desk and started mixing and learning these scratch techniques. With a four-track recorder I made my own demos, little mixes, just messing around. Then I joined a hip-hop band called Cut To Kill for two years, we even recorded an album but we spent the whole budget on the recording and had nothing left for releasing so that was a complete flop!

The Prodigy

The whole hip-hop movement is extremely articulate and forthright in its lyrics, so what pushed you away from using lyrics in your songs and moved you more towards dance music?

Well, you don't need lyrics for the dance floor that complicate matters. You need simple clever things that play on your mind. Don't get me wrong, there are some really good songs out there with lyrics in, but I never really got into that. When I was in Cut To Kill I even wrote some lyrics, but I was never that keen.

Did you have the dance floor specifically in mind when you started writing early Prodigy material?

What actually attracted me to it all was hearing Acid records for the first time. Before that, in the hip-hop band the lyrics were a big part, but as the band's DJ my role was primarily the music and I gravitated towards that more and more. I was always interested in breakbeats and the music side much more. Then I heard these Acid records and they were so simple. They could control a whole dance floor with just a few beats and a bass line. I went to this club and I could see the energy and the buzz this music was creating. It was like nothing I'd ever seen before. Everybody was happy and people were going around meeting new friends and I really liked it, so I started going every week. The club was The Barn in Braintree where Mr. C from the Shamen used to DJ, and they'd play stuff like Renegade Sound Wave's 'The Phantom', Patti J's 'Right Before My Eyes', key tunes that ranged from house to techno to the beginning of almost the breakbeat thing where the beats weren't normal techno beats, they were more shuffly, they had a breakbeat on there but they were slow. That was similar to the hip-hop scene – people were borrowing from the hip-hop scene and using it in this exciting new way. It had the same rhythms but with this essential simpleness – you'd listen to it at home and there would be nothing to it, in fact it would be so repetitive, but in the club that element worked really well. It became clear to me then that you don't need lyrics to make people dance.

So what is the most important aim in writing a song for you?
To touch an emotion. Whether it makes you feel happy or sad or whatever, it has to have a feeling. When I listen to those songs I love it. For example, *Ill Communication* by the Beastie Boys has a track on there ['Eugene's Lament'] which uses these fiddles all over the place and when I was listening to it in darkness in my room, it hit that mark. When I write I have to make the track hit that mark, give me that buzz, that tingle almost. When I come up with a sound or a riff and it has that effect on me then I know it's working.

How specific is that when you are writing – if you are writing a sombre track can you focus in on one incident or experience and use it for that effect?
Not really, it is much more general. You hear the sound and it is a whole atmosphere for the entire song, it is not that specific.

So you've never written a song with a specific event in mind?
Not really, it's more scenes than events, setting the scene

for people. There's a track on *Jilted Generation* called '3 Kilos' for which I pictured this smoky room with a whole load of people in there, very laid-back, a whole smoky vibe. That was the picture and I could hear the music that went with it. Quite a lot of the tracks I write are like that. In that sense I write somewhat like an ambient artist, I see pictures in my head and then put music to those pictures. There's another track on the album called 'Claustrophobic Sting' which is one of three tracks in a concept piece called 'The Narcotic Suite' which is all about the whole drugs scene. The first track is the one I just told you about, the smoky room, then the second has a whole up-lifting, rush feel to it called 'Skylined'. Then the last track, 'Claustrophobic Sting', is a real paranoid, 'depths of hell' track, although it's not screaming hardcore, it has some control on it and is still quite ambient in a way. The entire sequence was all pictures to me. You see, when people say ambient they think of Aphex Twin and The Orb, real nice floaty sounds, but ambient is just music that creates atmospheres, music for a certain picture. That is why I would really like to get into soundtracks, it seems highly appropriate to the way I write. The track 'Speedway' is like a soundtrack, the way it is programmed sounds as if these motorbikes are flying out at you, the sounds I have used create this picture. Music for me is a very visual form.

So would you say your writing is more of an environmental thing?
Yes, absolutely right.

So how many of these environments and atmospheres do you repeatedly come back to for songs, and what are they?
That's hard to say, there is really no way to pin-point that. I will come across a sound and it either hits the mark or it doesn't. When I wrote 'Weather Experience' on the first album for example, the strings evoked a whole scene, the real zen outside of things. It just happens.

Have you ever written a love song?
Well, it depends what you mean by a love song. For me it isn't a lyrical love song, but more of a mood thing.

Okay, so within those parameters have you ever written what you consider to be a love song?
I suppose the strings on 'Weather Experience'. They have a whole wide open welcoming sound, not really a love song but a really emotional sound.

That was a stand out track on the album, an exception. What was the idea behind that?
Well, basically I looked at the album and thought, 'Well, all this stuff is kicking, but that's it, there's no diversity.' For a first album you can't afford to be too diverse. The people who buy that record have probably bought all the singles and won't expect too much change. But with the second album they will expect something a bit wild.

Can you force a song if you haven't written for a while?
No, not at all. I did that on the second album, I went through a couple of tracks then dried up and I thought

The Prodigy

'Fuck! Where am I going to get the rest of the album from?' So I fucked the whole thing off for a month and just spent a lot of time listening to loads of other music. The Beastie Boys, Rage Against The Machine, Floyd, Senser, ambient, getting loads of inspiration from stuff that was so far away from what I was doing. One of the most inspirational records I have is the *Flash Gordon* soundtrack by Queen, which will probably sound really stupid. I don't like the single, 'Flash, ah ha' and all that bollocks, but the rest of the album is amazing. I listened to that so many times, it inspired me so much. All the incredible detail and the little pieces of music are so brilliant, that is a real ambient album.

So your writing is very visual. How do you transform the picture in your head into an actual song?
Well, that's not the only way I write, I have various ways of approaching things, and on this second album I was very eager to try some genuinely experimental stuff. There are various ways of writing. Take 'Start The Dance' for example, that is just a real hard club song, it didn't set a picture other than a hard club! (laughs) It wasn't a visual song, it was a simple song that had the right effect.

What are the actual mechanics of writing a song for you then?
I guess I would spend a week messing around with sounds, and I am really into weird chord arrangements and chord progressions. I like to do the unexpected, and I guess that is where my piano playing comes in handy, because I think I might be able to hear melodies and chords that others might not be able to. If I have a bass

line I will usually be able to hear the necessary details over that fairly quickly.

Some of the people I have spoken to have said that this technical ability can make you dry of any innovation though?
I totally agree – some of the tracks don't need to be musical at all, they need that random yet programmed feel about them. Some of the techno tracks that come out can't really be written down musically, and there's absolutely nothing wrong with that. I guess some of my tracks reflect that, although with the more musical stuff, which is mainly the new album, I do use that technical background.

Is it important to listen to music outside of your own genre?
I have never just listened to one style of music, never just techno or house, but it has always been predominantly underground, street level music, whether that be ambient or reggae or whatever, but not the chart stuff. I can't just listen to dance music all the time.

Do you keep ideas that are not working?
Yes, I'll keep anything that I can't fully use. I have a whole pile of material, sounds mostly, that I will keep for about a month, and then come back to it. Alternatively I will adapt that idea to something new I am working on.

How high is your productivity – if you get ten ideas how many tracks will you finish?
Probably about eight or seven. I'm not one of these people who apparently have thousands of tracks

unfinished that will never come out, but there are some that never make it to the finished stage. I don't give up that easily or that often.

How much do you feel in control of the whole songwriting process – what if it dried up tomorrow and you couldn't write another track?

I don't think you can afford to think like that, it would make you so paranoid. Besides, I get inspiration from so many things. It's really weird and I can't easily explain it, I can't pin-point one area that inspires me. We travel all over the world and we hear so much music; 80% of it is bollocks but there are some really stand-out tracks that I hear that might inspire me to search for that type of sound next.

So once you have heard that would you plagiarise or mimic that sound?

No, never. I don't make tracks that sound like other songs. I try and achieve sounds that have a similar feel. I heard a track called 'Gravitational Arch of 10' [by Vapourspace] which has a wicked ambient introduction of about three minutes before the beat kicks in. That gave me a really good feeling when I heard it in the club so I worked on some stuff that had a similar effect. Musically it was a totally different result, but it had the same feel. So yes, I do feel in control of the process. Essential to that creativity is the fact that with The Prodigy I don't feel tied to any one style of music which would severely restrict me. If the second album had been the same as the first I would have been struggling, all fast breakbeat kicking hardcore, then I would really worry about burning out from a lack of scope. Whereas all I care about now is writing music that I like. I am gradually expanding as I hear all these totally different styles, and that gives me so much more scope.

Is that the attraction for you with PWEI, because they have crossed so many different styles? Their first album was Ramones-ish then the next one sounded like the bastard sons of the Beastie Boys.

I do like that approach. The Prodigy has always strived to be different with each new offering. Visually we have had different videos for example every time. I think the turning point for me was when we released 'One Love'. Up until then we were full-on breakbeat and everything that rave stood for. But at that time rave was confused, it didn't know where it wanted to go. Should it go commercial or should it stay underground? I didn't want to get trapped in the war between those two schools of thought. So we started doing different things, playing less gigs in the UK, miles more abroad, playing college parties to people who wouldn't normally go to a rave so that they could appreciate us for what we are rather than as part of the rave scene.

How did the track 'Their Law' come about with PWEI?

I had originally gone to Senser but they were on tour and couldn't do it. We had played with PWEI a couple of times and I love the energy of guitar bands on stage. I think that guitar and techno could go together perfectly so well, but I don't think that anybody has done that well enough yet. Jesus Jones tried but that was always going to be more pop-dance rather than the harder stuff I want.

Do you think PWEI are the best offering of that so far?
No, I think Senser are. For me they are the best new thing to come out of England for a long time. They are better than Rage Against The Machine any day. I have respect for them because they have their own sound, Their music is guitar music with a touch of techno. What I am trying to achieve with some tracks is the converse, techno with a touch of guitar music. But it wasn't a case of Senser can't do it, who's second best, no way. We respect PWEI just as much and they were well into it.

How much do you think you will change to accommodate that genre? Maybe in twelve months you will have a guitar on stage?
Well, we've already discussed that idea funnily enough. You have to be so clever with the way you introduce new things though. You see, most of our followers are people who are into dance or have had something to do with the whole rave scene. The guitar scene is a totally different thing, a separate environment, and there aren't many bands using guitars in the dance scene that have broken through. I'm not about to suddenly think we are a guitar band. We are just trying to do different things. For example, if someone had told me a year ago that I would do a track with PWEI, I probably would have laughed, but things change.

So you're wary of falling between two stools and not being accepted by either market.
Yes, but rather more specifically, we are wary of not being accepted by our own market. Guitar music is not our market. That is great if those people like us, but if our own market doesn't like us anymore we are struggling.

But doesn't that insinuate that you are writing for a market?
No, absolutely not. The total first priority is to write for yourself and to write music that you are totally happy with. At the same time you have to get a balance, so that it is original but fits in a certain range, without trying too much experimentalism in one go, which would turn people off completely. All the people who were into the original Jesus Jones are probably not into all the dance stuff they do now, there was too much change too soon really, and that has jeopardised their fan-base. We are still based in the same roots as when we started, it's still hard and aggressive and has that same feel, but at the same time it experiments within that range as much as possible.

Of the lyrics that you do use, what makes you decide a track needs that?
The track with the PWEI is a good reference point. I have always said that we are not a political band, but this is just one point that cannot go untouched, this whole law about partying is such bollocks. How can any government tell young people that they can't go out? Powers to search and disperse and all that bullshit. I wanted one track where that point was put across, and although it is aggressive musically I wanted to be able to

put it across with more lyrics, much more vocally. It was essential to have the point made crystal clear. The problem then is that the lyrical articulation, by definition, will automatically and completely take it out of the rave scene.

Do you think that your emphasis on live shows is essential to your success?
Yes, absolutely.

Was that quite deliberate?
Completely. For sure. That is the way we have built the band up. When we first started we'd watch N Joi and some Adamski – N Joi in particular had that correct look for a live techno act. They had the control and the sound, and they had the total involvement and attention of the crowd. That is why we have four members in the band, there's something going on all the time. Fast dancing, good music, a real live performance.

Is that the main reason why you have shaken off that rave tag?
It has helped a lot, yes. We play festivals and colleges and the normal rock band routes, so that we can stand up as a working, gigging band rather than as a product of the rave scene like SL2 for example. We were like that ourselves up until a year and a half ago, but now we are strong enough to stand up on our own.

How much of your work is inter-related?
To a certain extent, some of it is yes. *Jilted Generation* is half following on from *Experience*, whilst the other half is

totally new. A lot of the ideas I have never touched on before. There's also stuff on there that I touched on when I was into hip-hop – 'Poison' is only 104 bpm, which is really laid-back and far mellower than I would have thought I would write, real down-tempo. I haven't written anything that slow since my hip-hop days. I really enjoyed writing that song and it is a stand-out track for me. It is a mix between hip-hop and techno and there's also our MC Maxim on there. It's not all lyrics though, I just don't believe in that approach for dance music.

So what was the stuff that was inter-related?

Well, I suppose 'Break And Enter' is a good example. It had the feel of the rhythm section of 'Charly' but still very different. The beats are similar, I suppose it would have been what I could have done if I had re-mixed a long version of 'Charly'. 'Break And Enter' is much longer though, a real build up but with the same flavour, a typical Prodigy tune but with a bit more. On *Jilted Generation* we tried to steer away from ragga too much because that worked on the first album and was okay for that era, but things move on and you have to adapt.

Give me an example of a song where you have used a trick of the trade?

The female vocal on 'Start The Dance'. That song was originally 150 bpm as a hard techno song. Then it went to 130 bpm for the US mix but that didn't work at all. So for the single we put it back faster. I almost felt like I had let myself down by putting that female vocal on it. It was such a fine line, and I wasn't sure if it worked or not. If I think something is no good musically but will sell, I absolutely will not use it. It's a fine line though between working and selling, and with 'Start The Dance' there was always a lingering doubt in my mind. It was almost too catchy to use. The same happened with 'Out Of Space', but at the time that was released there were a lot of similar things around. As far as catchy vocals go that 'Start The Dance' track is the last time I will release anything with that style of vocal on it. You can be a lot more creative than that with vocals – as far as most hands-in-the-air-and-catchy-female-vocals go, that is pure obvious crap and I am not about obvious records. You have to push yourself to be more creative and not be obvious, not to use too many of those tricks.

Where do you get your samples from?
Really strange places. My manager lent me all his hundreds of rock records and there is loads of stuff on there for example. Too many people use samples and just take a chunk of a record, loop it around and put a beat over it, but that just shows that no matter how much technology you have, you still have to be creative with it. Technology is only as creative as you are prepared to be. It's best when you change a sample, and place it totally out of context from the original use, that's creative.

What is the most forbidding track you have ever written?
Probably, 'Claustrophobic Sting', the paranoid section of 'The Narcotic Suite'. It's very heavy and abstract. My friend told me it was like driving down this black tunnel with spikes sticking in you all the way, ripping

through your skin and that was a great summary of that track, and I can give him respect for that.

So would that be part of the 'darkness' scene?
No, those terms are all so transitory, just useless semantics. The darkness scene as it exists in the breakbeat scene is just another phase people are going through. Jungle is another example. I would never categorise my music that way. The darkness sound is now going out of fashion anyway, although most of it was clichéd in the first place. You can't write a track to fit into any scene, you have to just write it to what you want, what you are about. Having said that, songs can evolve from scenes – in some aspects, I suppose our first album evolved from a scene, but that scene has died now and we don't have to worry about that.

How much do you rely on technological innovation?
I don't like to get bogged down with it all to be honest. I still use basically the same set up as I did when I started. I use a 16-track desk rather than Q-Base which has 64 tracks, which most people use. You lose the wood for the trees so easily with technology, and I have seen too many bands do that.

What is the most autobiographical song you have ever written?
Probably 'Poison' I guess. Hip-hop was the first style of music I was really into, and that track has a lot of that element in it, it sums up that portion of my life very well. Musically it represents the biggest chunk of my life I suppose, it is basically a hip-hop memory of all the stuff

The Prodigy

I was into, even though it is not a true hip-hop track.

How do you react when people call you the first star of techno?
I hate it, I don't like it. I didn't like it when *Mix Mag* put me on the front cover and called me 'Rave's Last Hope'.

Was that the same magazine who said that your 'Charly' track killed rave?
Yeah, and that was pretty bad as well! (laughs). That was a load of bollocks. I didn't kill rave, the shit that followed 'Charly' killed it, sampling kids programmes with a looped sample and all that shit. As for 'Rave's Last Hope', I don't want to be involved in that. I am not a spokesman for rave, we are The Prodigy and that's that. I am not a star and I don't want to let people down because I cannot be that type of person. There are very few stars in the traditional mould in the dance scene.

Is that why you are reluctant to be photographed?
Yeah, we are very careful. We have had seven hit singles and a hit album but even so you have to be careful how you present yourself. I don't like the pop magazines like *Smash Hits*, they would categorise us instantly and then those labels are very detrimental to the band's progress.

What is the most important record in your life?
Difficult one that. If I was forced to name any one, I would have to say the *Flash Gordon* soundtrack, for the reasons I mentioned earlier. Inspirational. But there are so many others, key tunes that were instrumental to my development. Early on, there were loads of tracks that

affected me – that group of records I mentioned that made me decide to get into all this in the first place included stuff like Renegade Soundwaves' 'The Phantom' and Meat Beat Manifesto's 'Radio Babylon'.

Who has influenced you greatly over a short period of time?
I can honestly say no-one. I don't get influenced by people, I get influenced more by atmospheres, surroundings and feelings.

What, in your terms, is success?
Success is being happy in your mind that you have achieved your own goals.

Liam's Suggested Tracks:

1. 'Poison' Basically this sums up the musical roots of myself, the hip-hop where we started. We go through different stages and that represents this stage well.

2. 'Your Love' was the B-side of 'Charly', a piano-driven emotional breakbeat tune that was uplifting but still hard.

3. 'Voodoo People' was an achievement for me. I went out of my way to do something different and this track achieved that.

DISCOGRAPHY

Since this book was written, there have been many reissues and remixes of the key tracks. The following discography is offered as a very simple contemporary guide to the major releases during these early years.

SINGLES

Feb 1991   **What Evil Lurks**/We Gonna Rock/
Android/Everybody In The Place
12" XL XLT 17

Aug 1991   **Charly**/Charly (Original mix)
7" XL XLS 21

Aug 1991   Charly (Alley Cat Mix)/Pandemonium/
Your Love/Charly (Original mix)
12" XL XLT 21 also on CD XLS 21

Dec 1991   **Everybody In The Place** (Fairground edit)/
G-Force (Energy Flow)
7" XL XLS 26

Dec 1991   Everybody In The Place (Fairground
remix)/Crazy Man/G-Force (Energy Flow)/
Rip Up The Sound System
12" XL XLT 26 also on CD with added track
Everybody In The Place (Fairground edit)
XLS 26 CD

Sep 1992	Charly (Beltram Says mix)/Charly (Alley Cat mix)/Everybody In The Place (Dance Hall version)/Everybody In The Place (Fairground mix) Your Love (The Original Excursion)/ G Force (Part 1) CD US Elektra 7559-66411-2
Sep 1992	**Fire** (Edit)/Jericho (Original version) 7" XL XLS 30
Sep 1992	Fire (Burning version)/Fire (Sunrise version)/Jericho (Original version)/Jericho (Genaside ll remix) 12" XLT 30
Sep 1992	Fire (Edit)/Jericho (Original version)/ Fire (Sunrise version)/Jericho (Genaside ll remix) CDXL XLS 30 CD
1992	Fire (Edit)/Jericho (Original version)/ Fire (Sunrise version)/Jericho (Genaside ll remix)/Pandemonium CD US Elektra 7559-66370-2
Nov 1992	**Out of Space**/Ruff In The Jungle Bizness (Uplifting Vibes remix) 7" XL XLS 35
Nov 1992	Out of Space (Original mix)/Out of Space (Techno Underworld remix)/Ruff In The Jungle Bizness(Uplifting Vibes remix)/Music Reach (1 2 3 4) (live) 12" XL XLT 35 also on CD XLS 21

1992	Out of Space (Edit)/Out of Space (Techno Underworld remix)/Out of Space (Millennium mix)/Out of Space (Celestial Bodies mix)/Ruff In The Jungle Bizness (Uplifting Vibes remix)/ Jericho (live) CD US Elektra 7559 66346-2
Mar 1993	**Wind It Up** (Rewound)/We Are The Ruffest 7" XL XLS 39
Mar 1993	Wind It Up (Rewound)/We Are The Ruffest/ Weather Experience 12" XL XLT 39
Mar 1993	Wind lt Up (The Rewound edit)/We Are The Ruffest/Weather Experience (Top Buzz remix)/ Wind It Up (Rewound) CD XLS 39 CD
1993	Wind It Up (The Rewound edit)/Wind It Up (Tightly Wound)/Wind It Up (Forward Wind)/ Wind It Up (Unwind)/We Are The Ruffest/ Weather Experience (Top Buzz remix)/Wind It Up (Bonus Beats) CD US Elektra 7559-66318-2
Oct 1993	**One Love** (Original mix)/Rhythm Of Life (Original mix) Full Throttle (Original mix)/ One Love (Jonny L remix) 12" XL XLT 47

Oct 1993	One Love (Edit)/Rhythm Of Life (Original mix)/Full Throttle (Original mix)/One Love (Jonny L remix) CD XL XLS 47 CD
May 1994	**No Good(Start The Dance)**/No Good (Bad For You mix)/No Good (CJ Bolland's Museum mix) 12" XL XLT 51
May 1994	No Good (Start The Dance)/No Good (Bad For You mix)/No Good (CJ Bolland's Museum mix)/No Good (Original mix) CD XL XLS 51CD
Aug 1994	**Voodoo People** (Original mix)/Voodoo People (Haiti Island mix)/Voodoo People (Dust Brothers remix)/Goa (The Heat The Energy Pt 2) 12" XL XLT 54
Aug 1994	Voodoo People (edit)/Voodoo People (Dust Brothers remix)/Goa (The Heat The Energy Part 2)/Voodoo People (Original mix) CD XL XLS 54 CD
March 1995	**Poison** 12" XLT 58 and CD XLS 58 CD

ALBUMS

Nov 1992   **Experience**: Jericho/Music Reach (1 2 3 4)/
Wind It Up/Your Love remix)/Hyperspeed
(G Force Part 2/Char!y (Trip Into Drum And
Bass version)/Out of Space/Everybody In The
Place (155 And Rising)/Weather Experience/
Fire (Sunrise version)/Ruff In The Jungle
Bizness/Death Of The Prodigy Dancers
XL XLLP 110 also on CD XLCD 110

July 1994   **Music For The Jilted Generation**: Intro/Break
And Enter/Their Law (featuring Pop Will Eat
Itself)/Full Throttle/Voodoo People/Speedway
(Theme From Fastlane)/The Heat (The Energy)/
Poison/No Good (Start The Dance)/One Love
(edit)/The Narcotic Suite (3 Kilos/ Skylined/
Claustrophobic Sting)
XL XLLP 114 also on CD XLCD 114

ABOUT THE AUTHOR

Martin Roach is a Number 1 best-selling author with scores of books on music, celebrity and youth culture to his name. He gained a degree in Historical Research before establishing Independent Music Press in 1992.

www.impbooks.com

www.bestsellingghostwriter.com